YOU DON'T HAVE TO BE A SHARK

Also by Robert Herjavec

Driven: How to Succeed in Business and Life

The Will to Win

YOU DON'T HAVE TO BE A SHARK

Creating Your Own Success

ROBERT HERJAVEC
with John Lawrence Reynolds

St. Martin's Press ⚟ New York

www.stmartins.com

Designed by Patrice Sheridan

THE LIBRARY OF CONGRESS CATALOGING-IN-PUBLICATION DATA IS AVAILABLE UPON REQUEST.

ISBN 978-1-250-09223-6 (hardcover)
ISBN 978-1-250-09224-3 (e-book)

Our books may be purchased in bulk for promotional, educational, or business use. Please contact your local bookseller or the Macmillan Corporate and Premium Sales Department at 1-800-221-7945, extension 5442, or by e-mail at MacmillanSpecialMarkets@macmillan.com.

First Edition: May 2016

10 9 8 7 6 5 4 3 2 1

For Brendan, Skye, and Caprice—

May joy and laughter fill your days.
I love you with all my heart.

And for Kym,
who danced into my life to fill it with love,
warmth, and hope.
I love you.

Contents

Acknowledgments

Thanks to my collaborator, John Lawrence Reynolds, who once again helped frame my thoughts and experiences and express my deepest feelings and beliefs.

I also need to acknowledge the assistance of my great team at Herjavec Group, especially Erin McLean and Mary Sanders, who supported this work from start to finish. To George Frempong—the best salesperson and best-dressed man I know, thank you for your friendship and support.

I am indebted to Jennifer Weis of St. Martin's Press for her belief in this book and to Sylvan Creekmore and the rest of the SMP editing staff for their assistance and patience. My literary agents, Joel Gotler and Murray Weiss, were instrumental in helping make this book a reality. They are true professionals whose personal attention is deeply appreciated.

I would also like to thank the *Shark Tank* team—from the production crew to hair/makeup team to the executive group to the Sharks themselves. We love what we do and have been able to build an incredible platform to promote entrepreneurship from our "little show." It's been incredible working with you all for the past seven (I can't believe it!) years.

And to all the viewers of *Shark Tank* who took the time and made the effort to contact me and offer their compliments and good wishes—my gratitude is woven through every page of this book.

There are no shortcuts to anywhere worth going.

—BEVERLY SILLS, 1929–2007

YOU DON'T HAVE TO BE A SHARK

ONE

Learning New Steps on a Different Floor

The most common career advice American children hear from their parents is *You can be anything you want to be,* inevitably followed by, *if you try hard enough.*

Don't take it literally. Nobody should. Eventually we all encounter limits on our dreams. One of the most popular sayings used on *Shark Tank* is "A goal without a timeline is just a dream." Some limits are imposed on us by physical qualities. Example: never tell a sumo wrestler he can become a jockey. Others are situational, or as simple as geography; it's difficult to become a world-class skier unless you live near snow. And some are self-imposed, when we don't try hard enough to make our dreams come true.

The path we all follow toward success, no matter how we define it, is never as easy as *Just try hard enough.* It never was. Things are not and have never been that simple. Yet one of the biggest obstacles we all encounter in this journey is easily defined and, despite all we may believe, something we can all learn to handle.

It's selling. Selling your services or product. Selling your dreams to others. And even selling yourself to yourself, which for some people can be the hardest job of all.

You believe you can be anything you want to be? Good luck. But win or lose at that game, the skill you need more than any other is understanding the basics of selling, and appreciating all the ways you will benefit from it.

All through life.

No matter what you want to achieve or who you want to become, the ability to sell anything—including yourself—is one of the most rewarding talents to acquire in life. Why? Because it is universal. It is difficult to imagine any aspect of life that would not benefit from knowing and practicing the skills of making a sale.

It's easy to see the importance of sales either when standing behind a retail counter or pitching a billion-dollar sale of aircraft to the Pentagon. But it's more than that. Sales jobs are pervasive in almost every kind of work you can name. You cannot be an effective CEO if you can't sell your company not just to customers and shareholders but to your staff as well—those you currently employ and those you hope to employ. It's also hard to be a great engineer if you can't sell your project to investors for funding. And trust me—it's impossible to make a successful pitch to the Sharks if you can't first sell yourself to us.

Selling is not just an essential part of business; it's also essential in personal relationships, all the way back to teenage years. You need to sell yourself on a date, and sell your parents on the idea of giving you the keys to the car. Eventually you are selling your abilities as an employee when you have your first job interview—and every job interview after that.

So selling is the basis of any relationship, personal and business. Don't believe me? Watch any episode of *Shark Tank* and think about the sales job that is happening—or too often not happening. When someone who hopes to persuade us to hand them $100,000 can't come up with the information we need on sales figures or market size or competitive situation, it's a deal-breaker in most situations. Many of them get slammed for not being prepared, no matter how promising their idea may be. In other cases, however, we Sharks may actually help them along, suggesting the things we need to know, trying to move toward a deal.

What's the difference? Why do we knock some and encourage others?

The difference is sales ability. The ones whose failings we overlook engaged us immediately in their business concept, and their promise that we will make money from it. The others did not. So we look for ways to work with those who succeed in selling us and to get the others out of the studio ASAP.

Sales are the beginning of everything that business strives to achieve. Not the end—the beginning. This makes it far more critical to a successful career than many people recognize. It's also been suggested that the world consists of "natural-born salespeople" and everyone else—that good sales ability is as genetic as the color of your hair. Which is a bunch of nonsense, and I can prove it.

Much of my success in business is the result of selling gifted people on the idea of investing their future with me and my company, and selling prospective clients on the benefits they will enjoy by giving us their business. Does this mean I was a "natural-born salesman"? No, it does not. I was not a unicorn, either; both are equally fictitious.

I *learned* to become good at sales. So can you. And the first step is to get over your fear of failure and rejections.

Which brings me to dancing.

*   *   *

By age fifty, I had achieved many things in life that I could not have dreamed of as a youngster. I had built a number of companies from little more than an idea into major success stories and restructured a Silicon Valley firm to avoid bankruptcy. I was expanding my current technology-based business into a worldwide entity. Along the way I also managed to run marathons, write two bestselling books, become certified as a scuba diver, play in celebrity golf tournaments, and race million-dollar cars around racetracks at speeds approaching two hundred miles an hour, winning my share of first-place trophies.

But I had never danced. Never even gave it a thought.

Oh, I had shuffled around a floor a few times with a partner, but it wasn't really dancing. I didn't know the difference between a cha-cha and a Chihuahua, and the idea of wearing an eye-catching costume while performing a waltz or a tango was as alien to me as singing with the Metropolitan Opera. I could strap myself in a Ferrari and dive off the Great Barrier Reef, but if someone suggested I learn to dance at the professional level on live television in front of fifteen million viewers, I would have waited for the punch line. They couldn't be serious. Me learn to dance? In costume? On live network TV?

Actually, the idea appealed to me. Who wouldn't want to glide across the floor with a partner, making smooth moves to the music and looking great? The truth is, I was deathly afraid. I actually danced with my daughter at her graduation ceremonies, a father-and-daughter dance. I lumbered across the floor trying to look cool and keep from tripping over my feet. When the music ended I could hardly wait to get off the floor and sit with the other fathers who had been as frightened as me at dancing in public.

So when the producers of *Dancing with the Stars* invited me to participate in season 20 of the show, what did I do? I agreed. Immediately. Actually, I thought they were joking. I figured somewhere along the way they would come to their senses, and I would get the call telling me they had changed their mind. With nothing to lose I said, "Sure, why not?" But the call never came, and when I realized they were serious about it, I grew petrified. Yet, for a number of reasons, it was one of the best decisions I ever made. I realized if I could sell the idea of me as a dancer first to myself, then to my professional partner and the judges, and finally to the viewers watching every step I took, it would be in many ways the ultimate sales job. And I needed that kind of achievement at the time.

In fact, like so many things in life, my decision was all about timing.

The invitation arrived while I was dealing with the end of my twenty-four-year marriage. I had been separated for some time, but I was still suffering almost overwhelming pain and a sense of loss. No matter how you portray it, divorce represents failure on the part of two people. Where children are involved, it brings pain, trauma, guilt, and grief.

I wasn't accustomed to this kind of suffering. Hey, I was the immigrant kid who became a wealthy businessman and international TV personality, almost entirely on my own. Sure, I'd had setbacks, but I had always overcome them with a positive attitude and stubborn determination. I didn't just take pride in my success in business; I also *reveled* in it. Nothing was going to get me down, because there was nothing in my life that I believed I couldn't handle.

Well, I was wrong. The failure of my marriage proved to be more than a setback. I was not prepared for the emotional landslide that overwhelmed me with pain and hopelessness. I grew depressed and felt both lost and powerless. Everything I had done, everything I had achieved in my life, appeared worthless to me. Despite challenges within my marriage, family life had represented all that I had worked for and much that defined me.

Advice began arriving from a number of sources. With it came condolences, suggestions, and warnings. Of all the warnings, one from a friend who had been divorced a few years earlier knocked me deeper into despair. "Robert," he told me when I explained how much I was missing my children, "I haven't talked to my kids in more than two years."

It took me a very long time to deal with that. When I knew I would not be able to handle the reality on my own, I turned to a priest who was also a family friend. He listened to me with understanding and sympathy before saying, "Robert, we heal ourselves when we heal others." I had a long history with religion and God. Born into a Catholic family, I had been an altar boy for many years, but over time I had drifted away from the Church. It wasn't that I no longer believed; it was just that I had lost many of the lessons that were once integral and basic in my life.

I could launch the healing process, I was told, by volunteering to help those in dire need of assistance. Their gratitude would validate my existence as well as their own. It made sense to me. If I could help others, maybe I could also help myself.

"Where," I asked, "could I make this happen?"

The answer was "Seattle."

Two days later I was serving food to homeless people whose only possessions were the clothes on their back and whose dreams were limited to having a safe, comfortable place to sleep at night. We soon found our respective roles: I was the volunteer, and they were the teachers. Soon I had no time to feel sorry for myself and carry the burden of guilt around. I was too busy helping others, but not too busy to hear their stories. At the mission I was told, "Open your heart and listen to the stories of these people because eventually their stories will become part of your story."

I began to listen, and what I heard was both wonderful and incredible. I began to change—to heal—when I stopped seeing the environment around me and saw only the people.

The people I assisted and lived among at the Union Gospel Mission in Seattle taught me about love, about hope, and about understanding the needs of others. They also taught me much about myself. It was a powerful lesson, and I promised someday to tell our story—theirs, about everyone's need for care and compassion; and mine, about the way I was changed and the gratitude I will always owe to them. I'm including the full story later in this book not simply to fulfill that promise, but also to share the wisdom with you. It did not repair me, but it began to heal me. I had done many wonderful and exciting things in my life, but I will never forget the comment of a man who had spent much of his life assisting people in desperate need. "I have never seen anything in life as fascinating," he told me, "as another human being."

When my journey in Seattle ended, I returned home to plunge back into managing and expanding my business. I was better, but I was in no way fully healed. I wanted to continue the healing by finding ways to restore the satisfaction with my life that I had once enjoyed. In the beginning it was difficult, because I thought I had no new horizons to explore and no new worlds to conquer. I had used that technique in the past whenever my life needed a boost. Need something to do besides work? I'll train to run a marathon. Looking for another world to conquer? I'll sharpen my golf game and aim to win a tournament or two.

This kind of thing usually worked, although it also complicated my life a good deal. When my marriage ended, I took another route. This time I chose to simplify my life in various ways. Among other things, I believed, it would leave me free to focus on rebuilding my relationship with my children. So I abandoned plans to run more marathon races, put my golf clubs in long-term storage, and sold some of my exotic cars. These were big steps for me, but they were easier to achieve than I expected.

I still planned to expand my business, and instead of being easier this proved tougher—not because of something I had done wrong in the past, but because of something I had managed to do very well.

During my absence in Seattle, my company continued to succeed on a day-to-day basis, thanks to the team of exceptional people I had hired over the years. They carried out the duties that once had been mine to deal with alone.

I have to admit that I accepted this particular reality with mixed emotions. Being so selective in choosing members of my management team had paid off handsomely—so handsomely, in fact, that I discovered I was no longer quite as essential to the company as I once believed. This discovery wasn't quite as comfortable as the one that proved I was a pretty good judge of talent when it came to hiring key people. If getting over my personal pain relied on reassuring myself I was both essential and irreplaceable, it apparently wouldn't be to my own company.

I was still running things, and we still had impressive goals to reach as a company. But it was more clear than ever that we would achieve our goals not just by me, Robert Herjavec, charging up the hill alone like Teddy Roosevelt, expecting everyone to follow me, but as a talented, committed team sharing the same objectives in a positive working environment. I was forced to admit that all the goals I had set for the company would be reached by the team working together far more than by me alone.

When it came to dealing with the painful aftereffects of my marriage collapse, I felt like a victim of my own success. I was proud of my team, and proud of myself for selecting and inspiring them over the years. The team's success, however, wasn't going to soothe my wounds nearly as well as I hoped. Something was missing. I needed a personal goal as well as a business objective. I needed an "I can do that!" challenge like the ones I had tackled throughout my life in the past. I needed to measure my determination and willpower in a situation totally alien to me. I needed something to encourage me to stretch my belief in myself. But at my age, where would I find one?

Which is when *Dancing with the Stars* called.

I was already familiar with *Dancing with the Stars*. The show had been a favorite of my mother's, and I remembered her delight when we would sit down to watch it together. Mother died a few years earlier, and I still missed her. Whenever I thought of *Dancing with the Stars*, I would recall the glow on her face as she watched dancers compete in brief, exotic costumes that probably shocked her—although she never let it on to me—even while she smiled and nodded to the rhythm of the music. It was a favorite show of hers during the years she battled cancer, one of the few things that took her mind off the disease that ended her life. Mother would watch *Dancing with the Stars*, then turn and say to me, "Do you think you might be on this show one day?" At the time, it seemed as impossible as so many other things in my life.

We watched the show together for different reasons. Mother loved the beauty of the dancing; I savored the tough go-for-broke competition. Twice each year, the show held a series of ten competitions pairing teams of gifted dancing professionals and inexperienced celebrities against each other. The tension was always terrific. *Dancing with the Stars* aired live, which meant the dancers could count on no retakes, no edits, no second chances. If they fell and landed on their tush, the whole world saw it in the comfort of their living room and had a giggle at their expense. During these competitions the dancers could shimmy, they could sway, they could boogie, and for certain they could stumble. But they couldn't hide.

That's why, with memories of my mother's love for the show, and my need to prove myself in a totally different milieu competing in a totally different activity, there was no way I would turn down the opportunity. Aside from the fact that I had nothing to lose, I felt that somehow it might bring me closer to my memories of my mother.

Only after I said yes did I discover so much about the show that I had never known before. For example, I learned that each couple—the cool and experienced pros, and the stumbling and perspiring celebrities—did more than follow their dance steps. They were expected to create everything about the dance to be performed every week. Each couple chose the dance step; selected the appropriate music; created the setting and story line; picked the costumes and props to wear; and, after a solid week of rehearsing, appeared at the studio ready to strut their stuff. Or not. That was the original idea, anyway. In reality, the professional dancers made all the decisions and the hapless celebrities simply prayed they could learn the routine and perform it when the moment came to do it live in front of all those millions of viewers.

Pressure? It hadn't even started.

I began by reviewing what I knew about dancing seriously and not shuffling around the floor like I and all the other embarrassed fathers had done at our daughters' graduation dance.

It wasn't much.

I had some idea of what a waltz involved. It was danced in three-quarter time, whatever that was. And I had heard of a fox-trot, which I assumed was danced at the same speed of a fox moving through a forest or across a meadow. (I now know this isn't true; it's coined for a guy named Harry Fox who danced it in vaudeville a hundred years ago, or so the story goes.) Beyond this, I didn't know a samba from a sombrero.

It didn't matter to the producers. I was given three weeks to learn our first dance with the partner assigned to me by the show's producers. Not so bad, I thought. Three weeks should be enough time for me to learn almost anything, including a dance that took only one minute and twelve seconds to perform. A minute and twelve seconds? That would flash by in a few blinks of an eye— or so I thought. Then I discovered how long a minute and twelve seconds seem when dancing in front of about eight hundred people in the audience and fifteen million viewers at home. I also learned that after the first episode of the show, I would be given a week—one week!—to learn four totally different new dances.

I was familiar with the scoring system, thanks to those evenings spent with Mother in front of the television set. Judges seated alongside the dance floor rated each couple from 1 to 10.

Their scores were blended with grades from members of the television audience, who voted via telephone or the Internet. Each week, the couple at the bottom of the score chart was dropped from competition. The news arrived without warning to the losing couple live in front of the audience.

To some dancers, it was a total surprise. "Bring a packed bag with you to every show," I was advised, "because if you're dropped, you head right to the airport." I accepted that fact. But standing there with your packed bags in a room down the hall from a ballroom, waiting to hear if you'll be around for at least another week, is an emotionally grinding experience.

So in the midst of my personal trauma, I was risking personal failure and public humiliation. Okay, my mother had loved the show, but even that hadn't been enough on its own to persuade me to accept the invitation. It took two more things.

Number one: I saw the dance competition as a means of testing myself beyond the decision-making aspect of running my business.

Number two: Much of the challenge reminded me of all the ways I had applied selling skills to other aspects of my life. My goal was first to dance reasonably well, and next to sell my skills to the world. One was new and scary to me. The other was something I already knew how to do well.

Really well.

The idea of a similarity between selling and dancing may appear confusing. Dance competitions mean learning new steps, being prepared for unexpected events, and, in this case, getting ready to hit the road if you don't succeed.

Hmmm . . . sounds a lot like being a salesperson to me.

The thing that inspires people to tackle a career in sales or, even more risky, to launch a new business as an entrepreneur is the same one that drives dancers to compete in events such as *Dancing with the Stars*—because it's fun when you do it right; profitable when you do it exceptionally well; and exciting, either on its own or in competition with others.

Despite all the odds against me, all the new skills I knew I would have to acquire, and all the risk I was taking that might have led to an even more painful battering of my ego, I could hardly wait to get started.

Because I was a step and a skip ahead of all the other amateurs in the dance competition:

I knew how to sell.

And, as we'll see, I could perhaps sell myself as a dancer.

TWO

Everyone Is Selling Somebody Something

Selling is not only about making a sale to a customer or a client. At heart, it's also about persuading someone to see your side of things and reach an outcome that ideally benefits both of you. Some people misunderstand this concept. They think it's all about coercion and manipulation, when it really involves getting people first to see your side of things, then take the appropriate action. True, the same techniques can be used to sell you a car or a purse or some other item you may or may not need. But it can also help convince your child to eat more vegetables instead of candy. Like every other ability we may have, it's not the skill itself that is open to criticism—it's where, when, and how it's applied.

The magic about knowing how to sell effectively is that anyone will respond to a good sales pitch. Even Sharks. Each of us on *Shark Tank* has, at one time or another, used a sales technique on a member of the panel. And it often works when we want to take a deal away from someone else. But not always.

When Mark Cuban came on the show he couldn't help promoting himself as the owner of the NBA Dallas Mavericks. Through his first season on *Shark Tank*, Mark used professional basketball "shot clock" timing when he tried to pressure us to decide if we were in or out of a deal. This gave us twenty-four seconds to either go along with Mark's offer or reject it, which gave him an edge. It worked at first, but eventually the rest of us decided this wasn't a pro basketball game but a cool business decision, and by his second season on the show he dropped the idea.

Lori Greiner has used her own version. She once tried applying pressure to us by taking her checkbook in one hand and her pen in the other before saying to the pitcher—our term for the entrepreneurs who appear on the show seeking an investment—"I'll sign this check right now and give it to you," meaning the full amount the pitcher had requested. The effect was to take the deal out of our hands. This was powerful the first time she used it. The next time, we were less impressed.

Demonstrating our selling skills on *Shark Tank* is fun, but a TV studio is nothing like the real world, where you run up against complex issues such as building a relationship from scratch and identifying the wants and needs of prospective buyers.

I'm sure you understand relationships well, but you may need a clearer understanding of want versus need. If the two words sound as though they mean almost the same thing, they don't. They are dramatically different in a sales situation, and understanding the difference between them and the role they play in a customer's buying decision are a key to successful selling. "Want" and "need" identify different mind-sets, and each is satisfied in a different way.

Think of them like this:

Someone goes shopping for a new car. If it's to satisfy a need, he or she will study advertisements, read reviews of different makes and models, talk to friends about the vehicles they drive, set a figure for the maximum amount of money they wish to pay, and visit dealers (or scan the Internet) looking for the best deal on the car that most closely fits their need.

But if the car buyer's need is dominated by a want . . . and the want includes driving a Porsche or a Ferrari . . . the need becomes secondary. It would be wrong and foolish for the salesperson in a Porsche or Ferrari dealership to suggest that the customer should settle for a Ford or a Honda. They are there to satisfy wants, not needs.

Another example: If you need a new watch to tell the time accurately, you can choose a Timex or a hundred other brands. Less than $100 will put one on your wrist and you may never be late for a meeting again. But if what you want is a $10,000 Rolex, your need no longer matters.

Those examples are easy to understand, but much of selling involves needs and wants that are not nearly as clear-cut, and the product being sold is not nearly as pricey and complicated. You can probably recall situations where you went shopping for an item without knowing just what you needed or wanted. "I'll know it when I see it," you may have told yourself. But depending on the size and complexity of the purchase, you were unlikely to "see" it without the assistance of skilled salespeople. Their job is to identify and ensure that buyers understand both their needs and their wants, and assist in making the best choice for that situation. If in your "know it when I see it" shopping trip you returned with something that fit both your needs and your wants perfectly, you likely encountered a first-rate salesperson.

Before a salesperson can address a customer's wants and needs, a connection between the seller and potential buyer must be established. In fact, it's much more than a linkage; even when measured in moments, the connection can be defined as a relationship of sorts. It hardly extends into a BFF kind of bond, but it needs to be revealing enough to provide the salesperson with an insight into some corners of the buyer's life.

If this sounds intrusive or manipulative by the salesperson, it's not. It is, however, essential to the success of every qualified sale that is made.

Here's how it works:

At the close of the movie *The Wolf of Wall Street,* the lead character, played by Leonardo DiCaprio, is conducting a sales training course. He hands a pen to one of the young men hanging on his every word and says, "Sell me this pen." When the man stumbles, unsure how to respond, DiCaprio's character yanks the pen away and hands it to another man, repeating his order: "Sell me this pen."

The scene has become something of a party game. A pen or a drinking glass is thrust at a stranger who is ordered to "Sell me this pen/drinking glass/whatever." Most people respond by talking about the item they've been handed. "It's a very nice pen," they may say, "with a clip for your pocket and it writes with permanent blue ink and . . ." Or: "This glass is designed to be easily held and sits very sturdily on a flat surface without falling over."

The correct answer is not to talk about the pen or the drinking glass or the gizmo. It's to talk about the buyer, and what he or she expects from the product.

Before buyers need to know anything about the pen, the salesperson needs to know something about the buyer. So the response to "Sell me this pen" must be questions such as:

> *How often do you use a pen?*
> *Do you use it to sign legal documents and on other formal*
> *   occasions, or just to jot down notes to yourself?*
> *How long have you been shopping for a pen?*

All of these, you'll notice, relate directly to the buyer, not the seller of the pen. That's why none of the questions refers to the price that the buyer plans to spend, because that's a question more closely linked to the seller (*How much commission can I make on this sale? How hard should I work at it based on how much the sale is worth to me?*).

The buyer's answers may trigger new questions until the seller is prepared to say, *Based on what you've told me, I have a pen here that fits all of your needs, with a few special features you'll appreciate.*

The salesperson has done two things in this exchange. First, instead of jumping into a sales pitch, she has launched a qualifying session to match the buyer with the product. And second, as limited as it may appear at first glimpse, she has created a relationship with the customer, who recognizes that the salesperson knows enough to make a realistic suggestion about the product.

If this all sounds a little silly, that's because we're dealing with pens and drinking glasses, small and incidental things. But the basis still holds all across the spectrum of things being bought and sold. Change the pen to a house, for example, and the qualifying questions are similar—only the dollar value has changed. If I were to order you to sell me a house, questions would pop up in your mind immediately, including:

> *Where do you want to live—downtown, country, suburbs?*
> *Do you have a family? How many children? Pets, in-laws, parents?*
> *How many bedrooms would you need? How many bathrooms?*

Saying to prospective homebuyers, "This is a very nice house . . ." before having even the most basic understanding of their needs and expectations—and we haven't even mentioned budget yet—would be foolish.

Grasping the importance of creating a buyer-seller relationship as the first stage in successful selling is perhaps the most important key to understanding how the entire process works. It's essential to appreciate this stage of selling, because it dictates everything else that follows. It also illustrates how skilled salespeople can make a positive impact on their lives that has nothing to do with generating a healthy income.

Much of the secret to happiness in our lives is based not on our wealth or our status but on how well we read and deal with those around us—family, friends, colleagues, clients, bosses, and so on. When you're talking about making a success of a career, many people will say it depends *entirely* on that skill, and I happen to agree. I can think of many brilliant people, from engineers and medical personnel to musicians and mechanics, whose abilities were never fully realized because they had no idea of how to deal with others.

Most people understand the importance of this knack and try to acquire it. One of the bestselling books of all time was Dale Carnegie's *How to Win Friends and Influence People*. Carnegie published it in 1936, and it was still in print eighty years later after selling more than twenty million copies.

What made it such a success? It was the first book to teach readers how to get along with other people. Some of its chapters were titled:

"Fundamental Techniques for Handling People"
"Twelve Ways to Win People to Your Way of Thinking"

"How to Change People Without Giving Offense or Arous-
   ing Resentment"
"Six Ways to Make People Like You"

Soon after its publication, someone described Carnegie's book by
saying that the core idea "is that it is possible to change other
people's behavior by changing one's behavior toward them."

And I thought: Wait a minute—that's the basis of successful
selling. Which, in turn, is the secret of getting through life with
more successes than failures, more joy than gloom, more friends
than enemies.

Does this mean good salespeople enjoy a happier, stress-free
life than people in other professions? I happen to believe it's true.
At least they know *how* to do it more than other people. Whether
they apply it to their personal lives effectively is up to them. But
here is what all effective salespeople know in their job that they
can use in their lives without knowing Dale Carnegie from Carnegie Hall:

- *They know how to negotiate.* It's a skill needed and acquired
  when dealing with customers, suppliers, and employees.
  Negotiating involves listening carefully, evaluating vari-
  ables, overcoming obstacles, and reaching agreement, and
  doing it if possible without strife, personal attacks, and
  burned bridges. You may think it's all related to settling
  contracts and making sales. But it's also part of getting
  your youngsters to eat their vegetables and working out with
  your spouse whose job it is to clean the cat's litter box.
- *They learn determination.* The best salespeople still hear the
  word no frequently. Instead of seeing it as a rejection,
  they consider it a challenge. So much of life depends on us

not giving up on our goals, and many of us never learn how to do it.

- *They gain confidence.* Nothing delivers self-confidence better than overcoming obstructions to score a victory. It's not just key to making sales; it's also an asset in handling crisis situations, small or large.
- *They get other people to agree with them.* In sales, it's part art, part science. It's also vital in so many aspects of business and personal life, from getting a raise from your employer to changing your teenager's conduct.
- *They practice self-discipline.* Most employees in large corporations can sleepwalk their way through much of their workday from time to time and still take home their salary. Depending on commissions earned from your sales almost exclusively means that coasting through a workday costs you money, so you are always aware of the connection between performance and payment.

Not all of these qualities were part of Dale Carnegie's philosophy, but they're all part of being able to deal with life and avoiding various disappointments.

So, one more time: Does this mean that, on average, successful salespeople are happier and more satisfied with their job than other people?

It sure seems that way to me.

THREE

Classes in the College
of Bad Debts

Understanding how selling works and practicing the skills behind it can pay off for you in strange and unexpected ways. You can pick up some serious life lessons, like the ones I learned during my first full-time job after completing my formal education.

All through high school, I had no idea what kind of career I wanted. My only goal was to become "something," meaning someone who achieved great things for himself and for others as well. The best plan seemed to be a career in business. What business? I didn't know. But learning the basics of business operations seemed a good place to start. If nothing else, I thought, I might get to hang around rich and successful businesspeople, and maybe some of their knowledge would rub off on me. So in my last year of high school I was studying various business-related things, including accounting.

I must have been better at accounting than I thought, because my business teacher suggested that I enter an accounting contest for high school kids. I didn't win the contest, but, out of hundreds of entries, I won third prize. This was a major surprise to me, but not as big as my discovery that the prize came with a university scholarship to study accounting.

I would be a fool to pass up the chance, so the following September I was in a university and immersed in debits, credits, liabilities, assets, and dozens of other details that buzzed around in my head, leaving me confused. The only impact they had was to convince me that I might have had a knack for basic accounting but I sure didn't have any long-term interests in pursuing it as a career.

After six months I realized that whatever I might become in business, the accounting side would have to be handled by other people. To put it bluntly, I dropped out. My future, I decided, was elsewhere—somewhere out in the "real world," not in some stuffy classroom. I would get a job, earn a reasonable salary, and move on from there.

Of course, I would also have to tell my parents that their only child, the son of immigrants, would not be getting a university degree after all. They would be disappointed. My father would be more than disappointed, I suspected. He might be angry. But once I had a job, things would go easier for me.

About a week after dropping out of school, I was home in the middle of the afternoon watching television when my father returned from work earlier than normal. Surprised to see me there, he said in his Slavic accent, "Why you not at school?"

"Well," I stuttered, "it's a funny story. See, I decided I'd had enough of university. I'm dropping out and getting a good job. I can learn about business better that way instead of in a classroom. I'll work my way up in whatever business I find and make my mark on the world that way."

My father, who worked in a factory and walked two miles back and forth to work every day to save bus fare, stood looking at me for a moment. Then he walked to the sofa and sat close to me, which was a little scary because my father was definitely not a touchy-feely-hugging kind of guy. Dad looked me in the eye and said, "I love you. But you no quit school. You go back or I kill you, bury body in backyard, nobody ever find." Then he stood up and walked out of the room.

Dad was a very good salesman. It's not often that fear serves as a sales technique, but this time it worked. Boy, did it work. I was totally sold on the idea of going back to school. All buying decisions are made with a benefit in mind, after all. In this case, the benefit to me was obvious.

In reality, I didn't fear my father would hurt me. It was clear, however, that dropping out of university would hurt him and destroy the relationship between us. He could not imagine me not finishing university. I had already gone farther in school than anyone in our family, and he had sacrificed much to get me to that point. I couldn't let him down, and I may even have realized that not finishing school would have been letting myself down. So I would return to school and catch up with some night classes and summer courses. But what to study? I'd had it with reading accounting ledgers. If I were going to read anything I'd prefer interesting books, like a friend of mine was reading in her English literature course.

"You get a big novel to read on Monday," she said, "and you read it by Friday. Then you discuss it in class."

That sounded like my kind of education, earning a degree by reading interesting novels. I signed up right away, immersed myself in great books, and was awarded a bachelor of arts degree. Political science fascinated me, so I picked up a minor in that subject.

If I really wanted a career in business, should I have worked on a degree in commerce instead? Others have asked the question, and it's reasonable. After all, a degree in literature and political science is a good basis for becoming a teacher, but that's not the career path I wanted to follow. Had I made a mistake in choosing those subjects?

My success in business suggests I didn't. I believe a university degree should prepare you for all aspects of life, not just a narrow interest. The lessons of great literature and the ins and outs of politics all have value in business and elsewhere, and I believe my arts degree has served me as well as any business degree might have. I also believe that earning a legitimate university degree, in whatever subject, is proof that you can set a goal and achieve it. That's a mark of success in itself.

Still, I was faced with something of a dilemma after graduation. Teaching was not an option for me, and I could not walk into any business with my diploma in hand and assume it would get me a job on the spot. Yet I needed to find *something*, or my father would have berated me for not studying something more practical.

Back then, people really did look for jobs in newspaper ads under *Help Wanted*. That's where I saw a job opening that declared *No experience necessary*, which was all the motivation I needed to apply. If I got the job, I noticed in passing, I would be a debt collector.

I was hired. That's when I discovered that the job involved working the phones at a bad-debts collections agency, contacting people who are usually able to pay their bills but refused to do it. They are very different from folks who want to settle their debts but are unable to do so for various reasons, including bad health or simply bad luck.

Collections agencies are the scrapyards of the commercial world. Whatever business you're in—jewelry, cars, fashion, furniture, you name it—all the glamour vanishes at that end. And don't assume that all the people on a collection agency's contact list are down-and-outers or deadbeats. Many of them are steadily employed and living a large part of the American dream, able to pay their bills. They just choose not to.

My job consisted of sitting eight hours a day in a cubicle with a speed-dial telephone and the names of people to call. The unpaid debts had been outstanding anywhere from a few months to several years, in amounts ranging from a couple hundred bucks to several thousand dollars.

The goal was simple: contact the people by telephone and persuade them to pay up. It may seem simple, but it wasn't easy. How could it be? I didn't know the people I was calling, and they didn't know me. We never met, and we certainly never became friends. Yet I wanted them to send me money. What's more, I was not the first person to suggest that they stop running from their obligations and accept responsibility for the money they owed. Most had been hounded by people like me for months, or even years. They knew the routine, and most of them knew they couldn't plead bad luck or a failed economy.

No matter how well any business may be doing, or whether the economy is up or down, a percentage of sales is declared uncollectible; in fact, most large companies have a flat percentage on their books for bad-debt expense. After investing too much time and energy on their own to collect the money, companies want to be rid of the problem. By the time the collections agency receives information about who never paid for what, most of the standard moves to collect money have already been made. Without success.

That's when the debts are sold to a collections agency for a small percentage of the money owed. The number of names may be in the hundreds, and the amounts owed could total in the hundreds of thousands, but it was better to collect a few cents on the dollar than nothing at all, especially since the companies had already written the debt off as uncollectible.

It was up to me to contact the names on the lists and ask when we could expect them to settle their debts. Their usual response was to spin a story or two as an excuse for not paying their bills. Many stories were heartbreaking. In the midst of me scolding one man for not paying his debt, he managed to interrupt long enough to explain that he had suffered a heart attack, lost his job, and his family moved out because he had no money to support them. I was skeptical, of course. Then I checked him out and discovered he was telling the truth. A little later I called another man who gave me the same excuse—heart attack, no job, deserted by family. When I checked him out I learned it was all a lie—he had a good-paying job and could easily settle his debts. He just wanted me to stop calling him.

A lot of people, I learned, seemed to be having heart attacks just a few days before I happened to call them. Unlike the first man, most of them were lying to me. To them, it was all some kind of Wild West game where they were colorful outlaws outrunning the sheriff, which was me, one of dozens of "sheriffs" at the collections agency. I had no badge to flash and no six-gun to twirl. Just a telephone, a long list of names, and a stack of outstanding debts to collect before the day was over. Talk about being thrown into the deep end of the pool!

If you're thinking that being a bad-debt collector was not the best way to launch a business career, you're wrong. I learned a lot from that job, and some lessons—valuable lessons—stay with me today. What's more, I recently discovered that four out of five Sharks on our show *Shark Tank* have worked in the collections business in some capacity.

So a few weeks out of university, I found myself making telephone calls to total strangers and starting conversations that often ended in screams, tears, curses, threats, and hang-ups. Needless to say, I collected very little money on that first day.

When my shift was finished, I was ready to look elsewhere for a career. Despite my frustration, I decided not to give up quite so easily. I knew I wouldn't be spending my working life in the collections business, but I refused to walk away without making a serious effort to succeed. Plus, I dreaded going home to tell my father that I could not finish the only "business" job I started.

That night I thought about the basics of the business and what it was really all about. Then I broke down what I was expected to do on the job, how I was approaching it, and why it wasn't working.

The people I called owed money. Few of them disputed this. And many of them, I knew, were capable of settling their debts if they chose. Instead of paying up, they made empty promises or offered silly excuses—anything to avoid meeting their obligation. I knew what they were doing while they offered excuses, and they knew that I knew what they were doing. Eventually it ended with screaming and threats by one or both of us, which did not help get the job done.

At some point, I realized that my job wasn't about making threats to people. *It was about making sales.* If I could sell them on the idea of paying even a portion of their debt, I would make money for the collections agency. And if I exceeded my quota, I would earn a decent income for myself.

So I began researching the business, and discovered that collections agencies expect to recover only a percentage of the money owed. I also discovered that about 20 percent of the people on each list would never pay anything, under any circumstances.

If I could identify the 80 percent of people willing to pay at least something on their account, and if the "something" was more than 10 percent of the amount owed, I would deliver better-than-average returns for the collections agency. I would also get satisfaction instead of frustration out of the process. This seemed like a fairly low bar to get over.

As much as selling has changed in the years since I had that job—and it has changed enormously, as I'll explain in this book—a few rules remain. One is to focus energy on serious prospects, avoiding tire kickers and window shoppers. True, many of these people can be converted into buyers with a lot of skill and effort, but this wasn't going to work in the bad-debt collections business. With time, I learned how to identify the 20-percenters within the first few minutes of calling them. I would put this group lower on my list and go to work on the 80 percent I might persuade to open their wallets.

Whenever I called people I identified in that 80 percent, I went to work learning as much about them as I could. I avoided making threats or becoming angry at anything they told me. Threats and anger produced nothing. I wanted to learn whatever I could about their lifestyle, get a sense of their values, and judge their expectations. In other words, I was looking to build a relationship between us just deep enough for them to respond to an offer I might make.

Building a relationship with your sales prospect was not a new idea at the time. Using the technique to collect bad debts was a little radical, however. No one at the collections agency wanted a relationship with a deadbeat. They just wanted money. Demanding money is not among the most effective ways to build a relationship, so I took a different approach.

As soon as the person I called understood who I was and what

I was after, they would begin making excuses and empty promises. I didn't want to hear excuses and promises. I wanted to hear
something about the person on the other end of the telephone
line, and I would start prompting them to provide me with information about themselves. I might, for example, ask if he or
she had gone to college. My question usually caught them off
guard, which was good. They would assume that I wasn't treating them as outlaws after all, but as someone whose life interested
me. Instead of tossing some prepared excuse back at me, they
would pause to think of an answer based on truth.

If they told me they attended college, I would ask if they were
working in a field related to their studies, phrasing it like two
people chatting on a train or in a bar. ("Oh, you studied hospital-
ity services. That's interesting work. Have you had a career in that
business?") My point is that the roles had changed. We began
with me as a sheriff ready to corral an outlaw. Once we began
discussing college and careers, it was a different script. Now we
had a relationship of sorts. A weak one, perhaps, but a relationship
nevertheless. Things that would have been totally out of place just
a moment or two earlier became more acceptable.

With the sheriff-versus-outlaw scenario out of the way, the
two of us could find something to agree upon. That's when I
applied my "let's make a deal" tactic. "I'm normally not autho-
rized to do this," I would say, "but if you'll send me [here I would
mention a dollar figure equal to about half of the amount they
owed], I'll get my boss to accept it and we can both move on.
You pay me that much on your account today and I won't be calling you back."

I did not promise that the balance would be forgiven. Bad
debts aren't written off that easily. But now instead of me against
them, it was both of us against my boss. If they didn't connect

with the empathy route, they could boost their ego by believing they had put something over on me by paying just half the amount they owed. It didn't matter to me if people on the other end of the line would brag to their friends about the deal they swung from me, the hard-nosed collections guy *(This dude was looking for a thousand bucks, and I got him to settle for five hundred!)*. Bragging about it might make them feel good, but I would feel even better because I collected much more of the debt than the agency expected to recover. The secret was this: I made these people feel like winners instead of losers by making an offer that met their ability to pay.

At some point I realized that I was no longer a debt collector. I had become a salesman, selling solutions that satisfied both sides of the deal.

Did it work? Did it ever. After six months using this technique, I set a record for the amount of money collected by anyone at the agency during that period. When I announced that I was moving on, management made me a bunch of attractive offers to stay. But I decided my future lay elsewhere. I had nothing against the job, and I proved that I could do it, but it was time to move on. I have always believed that for me to thrive I had to be in a positive environment, and I found that it was hard to stay upbeat in a collections agency environment. It was time to try something different.

When I left the collections agency I took with me a lot of lessons about selling and about life. One of them dealt with telling the truth. Or, more accurately, not telling the truth.

Many people tell lies to salespeople because they want to avoid confrontation. It's easier to tell a lie than to say no outright. It's a sales prospect's way of being nice by "letting them down easily." They don't realize that avoiding the truth in these situations robs salespeople of the most valuable resource they have: time. I would prefer people to be brutally honest with me instead of "letting me down easily" when they're not interested. Then I can use my time to move on to the next prospect. Good salespeople spend their time wisely by investing it where they can find their greatest chance of return.

The idea that you can replace almost anything lost except the time you wasted may be an old tune, but it is still true. Maybe more true than ever these days.

When I bought my first corporate airplane, many people assumed I was buying it for luxury and maybe bragging rights, but they were wrong. It wasn't just an airplane to me; it was a time machine, a way of capturing valuable hours that would be lost if I were a slave to commercial airline schedules. It enabled me to leave and arrive according to my agenda and no one else's. I admit it—I am maniacal about time. We are all given just twenty-four hours each day, and I try to squeeze every drop of productivity out of each of those hours.

The idea of making maximum use of your time seems rather obvious, but many salespeople fail to pick up on potential customers who are hinting at "Yes" when they intend to say "No." Why? Because they have what I call "happy ears." Selling can be a negative experience; every salesperson is prepared to hear "No" from time to time. Yet while they may be prepared for "No," they prefer to listen for "Yes!" Being positive is a great attitude to have, whatever your job. The mistake many salespeople make is that they are so eager to hear "Yes!" that they miss the "No" in the customer's conversation. They're hearing without listening. Because they have happy ears.

Happy ears hear only happy things. Happy ears don't confirm what someone tells them. When clients say, "You have a good product, no doubt about it," happy ears hear "You have the order" and start celebrating. Good salespeople don't have happy ears. They remind themselves that reality is sitting right in front of them. So when they hear something positive about themselves or whatever they are selling, they don't tell themselves they are about to make a sale. They respond with comments such as, "Thank you for your confidence. Now, if I may ask, what is the next step? Will someone be issuing a purchase order or a contract? If so, when might we expect it, so I can follow up?"

This is not being "pushy." It's simply good business practice. The salesperson is grateful for the order (if there is one) and inquires about the next step (also if there is one) while treating the customer with respect. At this point, the customer must either confirm that a sale is imminent or explain that he or she has been misunderstood. Either way, none of the salesperson's time is wasted.

Here's the difference between people with happy ears and those without:

Happy ears celebrate too soon.

Professional salespeople celebrate when the payment arrives.

Understanding how and why people avoid the truth has proved valuable to me over the years, but it was only one of many lessons I learned at the collections agency. I applied them when I created my first business, which I launched with little more than my own ambition and energy, and built into a company I eventually sold for a very large amount of money.

That's how much the lessons I learned at the collections agency were worth to me. For you, the cost of the same lessons is the price of this book.

Hey, I'm selling you a bargain, right here.

FOUR

The Art of Legitimate Selling

Many people believe that a sale marks the end of a long line of actions. In their view, things work like this: A product is made (or a service is established); the product is shipped to a retailer (or the service is packaged); and a customer makes a purchase. End of story.

Wrong. The story does not end with a sale. Every part of the story *depends* on the sale. *The selling process makes everything else possible.*

Nothing happens in a company until somebody sells something. Right now, some young dude in Silicon Valley may be writing a piece of computer code that will perform a new and valuable function. In a few months you may hear that some venture capitalist paid tens of millions of dollars for the code and think, "Hey, there's a way to get rich quickly, and there was no selling involved."

If you believe you can make your fortune simply by writing computer code or using it to become the next Mark Zuckerberg, good luck. But that kind of success depends on the longest of long shots. This book isn't about long shots or any kind of gambling. It's about the reality of sales as a critical and often undervalued side of business. It's also about the ways that sales techniques are used (or misused) by people in many aspects of their lives. And by the way: somebody still has to sell that multimillion-dollar idea before the code-writing dude gets a penny.

Here's the most important fact you need to take away from this book:

> Eventually everyone is selling something to someone.

It happens at every stage of a business: lawyers file agreements to launch the new company; brokers convince investors to provide start-up funds; entrepreneurs attract the talent needed to run the firm; designers and programmers make presentations to management for approval to proceed—every one of those steps demands selling skills. Yet if you should tell these same people that, whatever their official title may be, they perform a sales function, they would be surprised. Some would even be at least a little insulted. "Sales?" they might say. "I don't do sales. I'm a manager / programmer / lawyer / investment banker" or some other title. Maybe so, but if they are successful to almost any degree it's because they applied some innate selling skills.

They—especially men—could also be surprised to discover that sales training may have started back in grade school. I'm talking about a demanding situation where the salesperson needs to apply charm and earn trust to persuade buyers to pay cash for an essentially frivolous product, often at a price higher than those of similar products sold in retail outlets. How's that for a challenge? And what's the product being sold?

Girl Scout cookies.

You may not have considered this sales training, but it clearly is. It's fun and raises money for scouting activities, but it also aligns the Scouts with many of the same activities practiced by grown-up salespeople.

Girl Scouts set goals on the number of boxes of cookies they plan to sell during their sales season. As adults, if they choose to become salespeople, they'll either set or be given similar quotas. The young women also learn to make decisions about who will be available to make sales on specific days, and who will fill in if one of the Scouts becomes ill. They manage money as well, learning how to give change and add their cash contribution to the sales total. Dealing with grown-ups on a business level helps develop their people skills, and dealing fairly with customers on a business level sharpens their ethical standards.

See? It's not just about cookies. It never has been. It's about relating with people, and finding ways for everyone to walk away feeling good about the sales experience.

So why are some people uncomfortable about being linked with the sales process? It's true that not every transaction is as easily made as buying a box of Girl Scout cookies. And not everyone on either side of a selling situation is as warm and friendly. Some—a small minority, but that's all it takes to give any activity a bad rep—are linked to an old and less than respectable concept like the one I encountered when I was twelve years old.

I was the only child of brave parents who fled Croatia, which was part of Communist Yugoslavia at the time. We left with two suitcases, a few dollars, and a lot of hope. My father claimed that we exited Croatia because he was a political prisoner, which sounded very exotic and dangerous. Later, when I went back to Croatia as an adult, I discovered he had been more rebel than prisoner. He hated the idea of working hard and not being able to get ahead under communism. He also hated not being able to speak his mind. As a young man he had gone into a bar, had too much to drink, and began saying unflattering things about Marshal Tito, the head of the Communist Party there. You didn't do those kinds of things under communism, and his words got him tossed in jail.

Reasonable people would make the connection between cause and effect. If you do one thing, something will happen to you and it won't be very nice. So you stop doing whatever it is that causes something bad to happen to you. In this case, my father's reasonable response to speaking his mind might be not to do so, especially in a crowded bar, where the secret police may be within earshot. But Dad, like many hard-driven and opinionated people, was not always a reasonable man. No one was going to tell Dad what he could say and who he could say it to, so soon after he was released from jail the first time he was back in the bar saying the same kinds of things. He didn't do this just once; he did it twenty-two times.

The twenty-second time they released him from jail he was given a chilling threat. "If you come back here again," he was told, "you will never go home." My father knew what they meant. Every Communist country had a place for "the unwanted." Yugoslavia's was called Bjelo Otok, a tiny, barren island about a mile and a half in area, off the northern coast. Anyone sent there was never heard from again—in many ways, they simply ceased to exist.

The warning worked. Dad gathered as many of our possessions as he could fit into a suitcase and, with a handful of money, led my mother and me across the border to Italy. There we boarded the *Cristoefero Columbo* and sailed to Canada. His first choice had been the United States, but we were unable to get a visa. I was eight years old.

Landing in Canada, we made our way to Toronto. The only job Dad could find there was sweeping floors in a factory about two miles from our basement apartment. He was qualified for a better job but he spoke very little English, which, to some people, suggested he might not be intelligent enough for more demanding work. He was, I know, a highly intelligent man, but he was judged according to his English vocabulary, which was limited. He might have sought a better job but he chose not to. I suspect he was pleased to be out of Yugoslavia and preferred not to jeopardize things by being difficult.

I didn't think about it much at the time, but looking back I can only imagine how hard it must have been for him and my mother. Dad was a proud man, good-looking with a deep, resonant voice. He was also, I should mention, a very good dancer. Back in Croatia he had been popular with lots of friends. In our new home he was basically a nobody. He had no buddies he could share a few drinks with in a bar. Even if he had those kinds of friends, he had no money to buy drinks for himself or anyone else.

He was content to have both freedom and a secure job, even if he drew taunts from other workers because of his poor command of English. His goal was that of most immigrants to North America: he wanted to provide opportunities for himself and his family that were unavailable to him in the country he had left behind.

As I said, he was a very handsome man who took pride in his appearance. In his imagination I'm sure he saw himself as a leading man in a movie, perhaps a Croatian Cary Grant, not a poor immigrant sweeping a factory floor. But he did what he needed to survive, and swallowed a lot of pride in the process. It was worth it to him, because whatever he lacked in material things he was now free to speak his mind. That, and the knowledge that he was working toward a better future for my mother and me, were important to him. In some of my darkest moments I think about him and what he went through, and the memory gives me courage to keep going.

My mother was gentle and loving, an ideal balance to Dad's hard-edged determination. Theirs may not have been an ideal marriage, but it seemed to work well.

So when I returned home from school one day, expecting hugs from my mother and questions from my father about the lessons I had learned, I was shocked even before opening our apartment door. I heard my father inside the apartment shouting in anger and my mother in tears, repeating over and over that she was sorry.

"What's wrong?" I asked when I entered the living room.

My father grabbed papers from the table and threw them at me. "Look at what she has done!" he shouted.

I looked at the papers while Mother cried from a chair in the corner.

The papers were a contract, signed by my mother, to purchase a vacuum cleaner. And not just any vacuum cleaner. This was the ultimate cleaning appliance for its time, the Rolls-Royce of vacuum cleaners, complete with every gadget you could imagine. We didn't need a vacuum cleaner of any size. We lived in a tiny apartment that could be cleaned with a few strokes of a broom.

I looked at the price. The machine would cost us hundreds of dollars that we didn't have. Adding the interest charges to the purchase price, it would take us years to pay it off.

"Do we really have to pay this?" I asked my father. I knew we were living paycheck to paycheck. Money spent for this useless machine meant we would have to do without other things. Some door-to-door salesman had ripped us off by taking advantage of my mother's poor command of English and her trusting nature.

"Of course we do," my father said. He reached for his jacket. "It is contract," he said in his broken English. "When you sign contract, you do what you say. That is how things work in this country." He stormed out the door, leaving me standing in the middle of the room and my mother sitting in the corner, still crying softly.

My father was correct. A contract was a contract, even one unfair to the buyer. Back then there was no cooling-off period for buyers, and few ways to deal with unscrupulous salespeople.

I did not know the vacuum cleaner salesman, but already I had mixed emotions about him. On one hand I despised him for his greed and dishonesty. He had embarrassed my mother, made my father furious, and left all of us poorer. On the other hand, I wondered how someone could knock on a door, introduce himself, talk his way inside the apartment, and walk away with a contract for more than a thousand dollars. I couldn't imagine doing that. I was still the shy, self-conscious immigrant kid, scared of his own shadow. Where did he get the courage? What did he know that people like me didn't? How did he learn to do it? Or was he born that way? The guy had skill and nerve in abundance. What he didn't have were scruples. He had to have known we didn't need the ridiculous overpriced vacuum cleaner, and we certainly couldn't afford it. Obviously, he didn't care.

Things have changed since then. Consumer protection laws defend people against high-pressure sales tactics such as the ones used on my mother. What's more, buyers are more educated and, setting aside language difficulties like my mother's, they tend to reject high-pressure tactics. As they should.

True professional selling has nothing to do with taking advantage of anyone, especially the way the vacuum cleaner salesman took advantage of Mother. Professional selling is a matter of finding ways to meet the needs and expectations of both sides. When the vacuum cleaner salesman walked out of our apartment with the contract in his hand, only one side's needs and expectations had been met—his. He needed to make a sale. My mother did not need a vacuum cleaner. That's not salesmanship. It's dishonesty. I don't tolerate that kind of deceit in my business, and you shouldn't expect to tolerate it as a customer.

Dishonesty of the kind practiced by the vacuum salesman from so long ago is fostered and supported by salespeople who subscribe to supposedly can't-fail methods of making a sale. Fortunately, these kinds of salespeople, along with the high-pressure techniques they practice, are fading from view. Customers like my mother no longer tolerate either the salespeople or their sales techniques. They know when they are being manipulated, and they reject it. Good for them.

A few salespeople absorb books that promise to reveal can't-miss secrets about selling that, once you know how to apply them, are like pressing a computer key. Hit *Enter* at the right time and customers reach for their wallet, their purse, their credit card, or a purchase order.

No, they don't.

It didn't take thirty years of experience in the computer-related business for me to realize that *people are not programmed.* No app exists that will turn a sales prospect into a customer. No *Enter* button will complete the sale when pressed. And no way, in the twenty-first century, can ancient sales techniques work with any assurance of success. As I discovered at the collections agency, successful selling of any product by any person depends on building empathy with customers or clients and focusing on a solution that benefits both sides.

There are no shortcuts.

The memory of my father's anger, my mother's humiliation, and the salesman's greed will stay with me forever. But it didn't deter me from understanding the importance of making sales if a business is to succeed. Instead, it inspired me to achieve success in selling not by exploiting the vulnerability of customers but by appealing to their intelligence. I would do this by tailoring my sales message to their situation, their needs, their wants, and their values.

That was the basis of my approach with the collections agency. I had no intention of making a career out of collecting bad debts. But I recognized the role of sales in every aspect of both business and life. I also enjoyed meeting people and putting a deal together. I applied both to build my business, which depended on selling outstanding solutions to very demanding customers.

Many business decisions I make today still involve sales. I sell my company's future to the people I need to help me reach new goals. I sell my current clients on new ways that my firm can be of service to them. And I sell my company's services to prospective clients who may be unfamiliar with us.

None of these actions is different from things that all entrepreneurs and CEOs do to ensure success. You may think that entrepreneurs and CEOs are somehow "above" the business of selling. The best of them are not. They understand that selling is not only a part of their job; it is essential to their success.

Every member at every level of an active and expanding company needs to understand that they perform a sales function in their work. I am aware of this fact every day I walk through my office door. The success of my business and the prosperity of my employees demand that all of us—including me—sell and promote our abilities to each other and to our clients.

My success as an entrepreneur is linked to enjoying the company of people I am fortunate enough to meet, and squeezing as much joy from life—mine and theirs—as possible. I'm a firm believer in maintaining focus and working to achieve whatever goal each of us sets. I'm also dedicated to the idea that the best way of guaranteeing my personal success is to help guarantee the success of everyone around me—staff; suppliers; and, of course, clients.

I do this in spite of the chip on my shoulder that was put there by neighborhood bullies back when I was an immigrant kid dressed in funny clothes and living in a basement apartment. Those guys, in many ways, were sharks attacking small and defenseless fish. Like me. I had few means of defending myself from them. Even if I had tried to fight back with words or fists, I lacked the physical size to take them on and the language skills to tell them off.

This inability to deal with these bullies created resentment, and the feeling remained within me all through my childhood. It's still there today. Fortunately, I never let it fester into anger. I decided long ago that the way to get even with bullies was to become so successful that I would neither care about nor remember any bad stuff associated with them because I was too busy enjoying my life. The chip placed on my shoulder by the bullies remains there, and I'm always aware of it. I just refuse to dwell on who put it there, and how.

*   *   *

I think I have proved you don't have to be a shark to succeed in business and rise to a sizable level of wealth and income. Because you don't.

The one thing you must be—in business and in life generally—is someone who understands the role that selling plays in so much of our lives. Sometimes it's hidden, and sometimes it's obvious. The trick is knowing how to apply selling skills without the customers knowing they are being sold. By "customer" I don't mean only the people prepared to exchange their money for whatever you're selling. I'm talking about friends, life partners, children, colleagues, coworkers, and everyone else whose trust and support are valuable to you. For any reason. Ideally, they provide their trust and support not because you want it from *them,* but because they want to give it to *you.*

So here's my definition of the perfect sale: the customer believes he or she has been in control of the situation, and has completed a transaction that benefits both buyer and seller.

And, when all goes well, they are entirely correct.

FIVE

The Chill of Cold Calls

In most situations, the buyer seeks out the seller. Whether visiting a retailer, responding to an advertisement, or selecting a product from a catalog, the encounter tends to be launched by the person who needs—or wants—a product or a service.

But one selling technique is very different. In this one, whoever is selling the product or service contacts buyers directly and unexpectedly. They do it by interrupting the potential customer's day with a telephone call, proposing a purchase the buyer was usually not considering at the time. At its most basic level—selling new windows or cleaning your furnace ducts—it's called telemarketing, and no means of making sales is less appreciated and more vilified.

Telemarketing, for all its annoying frequency, is actually a variation of direct mail, which fills mailboxes with flyers promoting a product. It's blanket-style advertising, covering a wide market area on the assumption that everyone within it is a potential customer. But, of course, not everyone is. That's why users of direct mail expect about a 2 percent response for all of their efforts and expense. If they send a thousand flyers, they will be satisfied if twenty people take the time to call for more information.

That's not very efficient. But then neither are telemarketers, who achieve a similar success rate with the people they contact by telephone.

This isn't really selling. Not on a professional, career-based level. Much of the telemarketing industry is tainted with questionable methods and outright fraud. For example, it's somewhere between amusing and infuriating for an Apple Mac owner to receive a call from someone claiming to be from Microsoft who is prepared to repair a problem on their Windows program.

There are occasions, however, when professional salespeople find themselves in a situation similar to telemarketers. This occurs when they set out to contact prospects and make an unanticipated sales pitch, or at least schedule a full sales presentation. Telemarketers, sitting among dozens or even hundreds of tiny cubicles facing computer monitors, are geared for rejection—often in the form of an insult, followed by a hang-up. No problem. They know they are more of a nuisance than a skilled salesperson, and they don't have time to deal with rejection. Their immediate response is to strike the keyboard and let the computer call the next randomly selected prospect.

For people whose career plans depend on a higher level of sales success, the idea of intruding in that manner is chilling. Like most of us, they hate being intrusive and resent having a few seconds to avoid a hang-up, and they fear being the target of the kind of wrath heaped upon telemarketers. So why bother? Because it remains the best way to reach beyond an existing customer base and bring in new buyers, who, it's expected, will become long-term customers. It's not restricted to finding ways to grow a company's sales volume, either. It's often just a matter of maintaining that volume over time. Mergers, bankruptcies, new competitors, and a number of other developments can rob a company of its long-term customers, so standing still really means going backward. Those lost customers need to be replaced, and companies do so by reaching out to snag new customers instead of sitting back, waiting for them to call or come through the door.

They do it with a process that used to be referred to as cold calling. The term recently has changed to outbound, which sounds more sophisticated and productive. Call it what you will, the difference between it and telemarketer calls is significant. Telemarketers assume the world is populated with people who want their product and service, and if they don't—hey, hit the computer key and make another random call. Nothing qualifies the individuals being called except access to their telephone numbers.

Not all calls to unqualified prospects are from people selling dubious products or services. Investment brokers and financial advisers are encouraged to make cold calls in search of new clients, a technique known as prospecting. It's a legitimate way to search for new clients beyond the referrals that brokers and advisers normally rely on to build their business. These should not be confused with "boiler room" operations like the ones featured in *The Wolf of Wall Street*, where cold callers make impossible promises of stock performances to greedy and gullible buyers.

Reputable brokers and financial advisers qualify the people they call to at least one extent. Using census records and other sources, they reach out to prospects who live in middle- or upper-middle-class areas who likely have sufficient income to invest in legitimate securities. Qualifying the prospect even in this slim manner separates telemarketing from outbound sales.

Business-to-business outbound calls qualify the prospect in greater detail, which requires the salesperson to do some homework before making the call. Some of the means of choosing whom to call are obvious. If the product being sold is robotic machinery for industries assembling cars and appliances, you don't call a clothing manufacturer or retailer. Digging more deeply, the target company's expansion and sales record may be researched, the most influential buyer at the firm may be identified and profiled, and factors such as location and purchase history could be examined.

But when all the preparation is done, you still have to make the call. And that's the scary part.

No matter how much you have qualified the person you are calling, and how prepared you may be with your facts and script, you are about to become an interruption to someone who is probably busy. Cold callers don't have the fallback position of telemarketers earning minimum wage who are accustomed to immediate rejection. On a business-to-business level they are trained professionals geared to build relationships and handle objections. Yet they are aware that, almost as soon as they finish introducing themselves, the prospect may well be thinking:

> *This person wants to sell me something.*
> *I don't know his/her name.*
> *I don't know his/her background or reputation.*
> *I don't know what he/she is about to sell.*
> *I don't have any relationship with them.*
> *I don't know how [whatever it is they are selling] will help me do my job better or help the company make more money.*
> *I have other things to do.*

If you're a salesperson making the cold call, you almost anticipate a "No, thank you" and a hang-up. You may be familiar with rejection, but in other sales situations you have a chance to make your pitch first. On cold calls, you may be lucky to finish saying your name. All failures carry lessons with them, but what have you learned when a prospect tells you to "Get lost" before hanging up? This is why outbound/cold calling is probably the least attractive assignment for many salespeople. Yet it is also a low-cost way of setting up sales presentations to new prospects if the caller can make a case quickly and convincingly.

All it takes is to reach out to a total stranger, put him or her in the right frame of mind, create context, build rapport, and obtain a commitment for a meeting and a presentation.

See why cold calling is perhaps the most demanding method that most salespeople face?

The best solution is to follow a script, or at least a fixed procedure. Either way, every cold call needs to achieve these in rapid order:

1. Raise the prospect's curiosity. ("Who is this? Why should I care?")
2. Provide context in a dozen words or less, also known as an elevator pitch ("We've cut energy costs for people in your industry by 35 percent.")
3. Ask for permission to continue. ("May I explain how it's done? It will take less than a minute.")
4. Confirm that the prospect is a fit. ("Does this sound like the kind of advantage you'd like to have over competition?")
5. Schedule a full presentation—date, time, and attendees. ("May I send you some material to explain the process before our meeting?")

Getting to step 5 is more art than science. Cold callers need a script and guidelines, but they also need to anticipate objections and concerns, and know how to handle them gracefully ("Did I call you at a bad time?" "May I send you the material and call you when you've had a chance to study it?").

Sending material or scheduling a later call is an easy way out for both sides. The prospect gets to return to whatever they were doing when they answered the call, and the salesperson has avoided an instant hang-up. Unfortunately, not much has been accomplished. The very best cold callers—they are a rare breed but they actually exist—know how to maintain the prospect's interest and build on it, ideally getting a commitment for a full sales presentation. How? By creating rapport and trust with a telephone call. They still experience failure, but hang-ups are not as frequent.

Many companies are providing their sales personnel with assistance through the use of customer relationship management (CRM) programs. The CRM approach is directed primarily at retaining existing companies by compiling information from a range of sources—Web sites, marketing materials, social media, and other places where a firm's activities can be tracked.

This sounds simple on the surface, but in practice CRM can become mind-bogglingly complex. They can be operational (measuring what prospective companies do and how well they do it); analytical (searching for cause-and-effect measures in data on buying behavior); and collaborative (combining data on target companies from various sources to create a well-rounded picture).

Existing Internet operations market their contacts to achieve the same thing. Large companies can use various devices including spin-offs of services like the business social networking service LinkedIn. With about a hundred million hits each month and twenty-four different languages, the amount of corporate information that can be gleaned from its postings is immeasurable.

Selling really has become that sophisticated. You need a giant multibillion-dollar company to justify all that effort and expense, plus a sales staff who can apply the information gathered and convert it into a completed sale. You also need someone who can interpret the bought-and-paid-for data, converting it into that out-of-the-blue sales pitch.

And that's the problem. Cold callers may be better armed, which may boost their confidence, but everything still depends on those few seconds between the moment that prospects pick up their telephone and the moment they realize they are being asked to hear or schedule for an unanticipated sales pitch.

Not many people are pleased about making cold calls, no matter how well armed they may be with data. Those who are, and who can finish their cold calls with a date and time for a presentation—or better yet, a closed sale—are in the elite class of sales professionals.

Just don't call them telemarketers.

SIX

The Biggest Myth About Sales and Life

Every profession has its stereotypes, and for years the one closely associated with salespeople has been a loudmouthed, poorly dressed extrovert who would sell his or her grandmother to close a sale.

There are many errors in that description, but the biggest—and the one that may be least obvious to you—is the word "extrovert."

The basic definition of extrovert is *someone concerned only with whatever is external.* This explains why extroverts seem to be at home in every social situation. They're not concerned about what anyone else is thinking or feeling. Their attention is fixed only on what they can see and hear.

So does this mean certified extroverts are automatically qualified to become successful salespeople?

Not a bit.

Based on the assumption that being an extrovert is essential to successful selling, it follows that you can't be quiet, reflective, and reserved and still score big in sales. That's a load of *sranje,* a Croatian word for something that has no value at all. Not even to a bull.

*   *   *

We hear a lot about schoolyard bullies these days, and how to deal with them. Everyone agrees that bullies should be either avoided or dealt with, whether they are found in schoolyards or boardrooms.

When I was in grade school, bullies were considered a normal part of life to young immigrant kids. If we complained, we were told to "suck it up" and get on with our lives. That's easy to say, but when you're the new kid with weird clothes and a funny way of talking, it's agony. There's no other word to describe it. You feel pain, you feel rejection, and you feel a lot of emotions, including fear and insecurity. And you never get over them entirely.

In my case, the taunts and beatings put the chip on my shoulder that I mentioned earlier.

The chip did not make me an extrovert. It moved me in the opposite direction. I grew quietly determined to prove to the world—and, I suspect, to myself—that I was not an object of ridicule, but a guy capable of doing things as well as anyone else. Maybe even *better than* anyone else. At times, my determination would get the best of me, suggesting that my ego was growing out of control. Whenever this happened my mom would say, "You are no better than anyone else, but no one else is better than you." The words have stayed with me. Whenever someone appears on *Shark Tank* desperately looking for funding and support, it never occurs to me to think, "I made it and they didn't, so I am better than they are." Because deep down I know I am not. We are different in personality, backgrounds, and assets, perhaps. But one of us is not "better" than the other.

When you think about it, my determination to ignore the bullies and get my revenge by succeeding in business was the only natural response available to me. I wasn't big enough to attack the bullies with my fists. And I couldn't put them down with words, because I had yet to acquire a large vocabulary in English or the ability to deliver it without a heavy accent. So I endured the taunts and put-downs and concentrated on developing my ideas and abilities.

I also grew to accept that I would never get anything from life that I didn't achieve on my own. My parents loved and supported me, but that was the extent of their assistance. They couldn't afford to buy me clothes as fashionable as those of the other boys, couldn't send me to a private school where the students were better disciplined, couldn't get rid of my embarrassing accent, and couldn't hover over me on the way to and from school. Nor did I expect them to do these things. If I needed comfort and reassurance when they weren't around to provide it, I would go to church. I served as an altar boy for some time, and listening to all those sermons over the years, one line was burned into my awareness: *God helps those who help themselves.* Whatever plans I might have in life, I would reach them only by helping myself get there.

Handling things on my own gave me another view of life as well. I couldn't expect anyone or anything to assist me because that would be a handout, and I didn't believe I deserved handouts. Neither, I accepted, did anyone else. The only thing I could expect from life was the right to prove myself. I still feel that way, with all my heart. Nobody owes any of us a thing, and none of us deserves more than a chance to become whatever our talents and ambitions can provide. We each get from life what we make of it.

Of course, some of us get a head start in life. Born into wealth and privilege, some are given the tools to learn and the opportunity to succeed in greater measure than others.

But so what? That's the way they get started, not necessarily the way they finish. I have run marathons, and I can assure you that the people at the front of the pack when the starter's gun goes off are not in the same position 26.2 miles down the road, when the finish line is crossed. Life is a marathon. We all begin from a different position, and our positions change throughout the race. The best we can accept is that we have the chance to move up while the race is being run.

The deprivations in my years as the only child in an immigrant family did not make me an extrovert. They made me persistent. I grew determined to succeed in ways that the bullies could never understand and could never match. Each time I reached a new goal, I grew more confident that I could set a higher goal and reach it, and when I did, I reached for the next one above it. I was never the smartest kid in the class, nor the best-looking, the tallest, or the strongest—but I was always the first to get up when knocked down, an attitude that, with one exception, I've maintained throughout my life.

I have also been generally confident in my ability to succeed, but being confident should not be confused with being extroverted. I may be confident in the things I seek to achieve, but am nowhere near as extroverted and blustery as my fellow Sharks Kevin O'Leary, Mark Cuban, and Daymond John. I am, I believe, as good a salesman as any of them.

Maybe better.

But that doesn't make me an extrovert.

I mentioned the challenges I faced as a child to underline my point that extroverts do not make great salespeople. Anyone so focused on themselves that they tend to tune out another person will never be as successful as someone who is sincerely interested in other people.

In the broadest sense of the word, the act of selling involves intimacy on a deep emotional level because so much happens beneath the surface. In the movie *Cadillac Man*, the late Robin Williams played a salesman who says "selling is as close as you can get to another human being without sleeping with them." I have never doubted the truth of that line.

The question still stands: Are some people "born" to succeed in sales? Is there something in their DNA that makes us say, "That woman could sell snow in Alaska"?

There can be, depending on the situation. Some have appeared on *Shark Tank,* trying to sell us on the idea of investing in their business idea. They have been effective enough—and their business plan has been promising enough—for some of us to close a deal with them. This doesn't prove that salesmanship is natural to some people, as if it were a genetic factor such as the color of their eyes or the shape of their chin. And it certainly never leads to closing a deal all on its own. *Shark Tank,* after all, is a unique environment lacking many things that professional salespeople must deal with in the real world—things such as direct competition and often complex decision making.

Even more than that, we Sharks aren't interested solely in buying what's put in front of us. We're interested in the opportunity to build a business that will thrive and grow over the long term, one that is likely to require our personal involvement in its management and expansion.

I agree that some people have an aptitude for writing or music or some other creative work. They are rightly referred to as "born writers" or "born musicians." When it comes to the art of selling, however, the biggest factor in determining someone's success isn't "natural ability." It's training and enthusiasm. If you have enough desire and energy, and follow the guidance of an effective mentor, you will amaze yourself (and the rest of the world) with your accomplishments. This works even if you have zero experience in selling.

Or dancing.

When I agreed to take part in *Dancing with the Stars,* I risked embarrassing myself in front of the world. I was used to taking various kinds of risk. For several years I had risked my life driving powerful race cars at speeds approaching two hundred miles per hour on tracks all over the world. One wrong move at that speed and I would have been dealing with something much more serious than embarrassment. After a nasty crash on a racetrack in Brazil, I spent some time in a São Paulo hospital reliving the experience of hitting an immovable object at high speed. Racing was fun, but dancing looked like it would be fun as well. Fun was something I could use at the time.

I agreed to be part of the show, promising myself that I would work hard, learn something new, and try to enjoy myself. This, by the way, happens to be a good attitude to have when launching a career in sales.

Learning to sell is a little like taking dancing lessons: you start with basic steps . . . carefully watch what the other person is doing . . . accept that any step you miss comes with a lesson to improve your performance . . . and when all goes well, you really enjoy the experience.

I'm not suggesting that if you can dance, you can sell. But hey—it can't hurt.

Back to selling.

The most attractive part of selling to me is the way it helps handle other aspects of life. At its heart, selling is effective communication between people.

I don't know any activity in life, from dealing with children to settling international crises, that doesn't benefit from the ability to get your point across to the other person. More than that, it helps you appreciate their needs and expectations. I honestly believe that everything worthwhile in life depends on that one skill. You cannot communicate effectively with anyone until you first organize your thoughts. And you cannot appreciate another person's point of view unless you listen closely to the things they are saying with both their voice and their body language.

This last point supports my view that introverted people can achieve spectacular success in sales. Why? Because they are better listeners. Extroverts often spend time talking about themselves and their concerns, assuming that anything that is not either within their view or value system doesn't count. Introverts, by nature, listen more accurately because they speak less frequently. We all need to sharpen our listening skills and apply whatever we learn to reach our personal goals. Sometimes the goal is making a sale. Sometimes it's finding a job. And sometimes it's persuading others that they should look at us differently—with appreciation, with understanding, and maybe with affection.

There are other benefits as well.

Salespeople tend to fly solo. They may have backup support—a sales manager, someone to handle financing, a team of marketing experts perhaps. But when they are face-to-face with a customer and they know—*when they totally, absolutely, unconditionally know*—that whatever they are selling perfectly fits the customer's needs, total control is in their hands. To people like me who love selling, the experience is exhilarating.

I'm not knocking the concept of teamwork in business. Team playing is fine from a corporate point of view. As a guy who built his company out of little more than vision and ambition, and who still takes part in every major corporate decision, I can assure you that teamwork is vital to our success.

But so is employee self-satisfaction. We all celebrate in our company whenever we achieve a major goal such as tying up a big contract with a new client. No one's enthusiasm, however, sails higher than the person whose selling skills made it happen. They were on the spot making decisions, handling objections, searching for solutions, and finally sealing the deal. It's not quite like winning a gold medal at the Olympics (I can imagine), but sometimes it feels close.

Of course, not every sales pitch we make proves successful. That kind of perfection does not occur for my company, for me, or for anyone else. We win and we lose, and the unexpected can happen at any time. We can be amazed to lose a contract that appeared to be a sure thing, and we can be surprised at an equally unexpected success. None of this affects our determination to score a win.

"So what happens," I hear you ask, "when you don't succeed? Do you sink as low with failure as you fly high with success?"

Not really. This is not a game where every loss is subtracted from your list of victories. Failure is never a disaster. I see it as a way of showing me how to improve, and how to work toward more celebrations in the future.

If you don't have to be an extrovert to be good at selling, and shyness doesn't disqualify you for a sales career, what qualities do you need to get started? I've identified four of the most important traits for good salespeople that I look for when hiring new sales staff. They're easy to develop, and successfully applying them becomes more natural with experience.

Here's something to think about as you read them:

Aren't they the same kind of skills that help each of us deal with the challenges we face in life, and the ones we use to create the happiness we deserve?

See if you don't agree with me.

1. They believe in what they do.

Great salespeople have a hard time selling anything they don't believe in. They have an equally large problem if they also don't believe in the importance of their job. Anyone who thinks selling is a second-rate career is doomed before they begin. Selling is a critical part of all business operations. This makes the sales staff as important as any department in the company.

Many years ago, I spotted a sign in a sales manager's office. The sign read, *Nothing happens until somebody sells something.* I remember smiling at the obvious wisdom of the idea, and the fact that I hadn't thought about sales that way before. It made sense. All the research, all the design activity, all the efficient production, and all the shipping and other goings-on in a company will stop dead if everything being produced is not being sold. Good salespeople are as important as anyone in a company, all the way up to the CEO. That's why top-notch salespeople are highly valued in every industry. And why, short of a total economic disaster, they are almost never out of work.

2. They enjoy the company of people.

Selling is not entirely an individual sport. Long-term success depends on a salesperson's ability to work well with support staff who take charge of things such as delivery, service, financing, and a dozen other tasks. This explains why selling can be such a challenge to some people—you have to be good at flying solo and equally good at being part of a team.

Not everyone can deliver both skills in equal quantity. Competitive high-caliber athletes are usually good at both, because they are familiar with the need to deliver maximum effort while depending on the contributions of others. It's not totally necessary to be athletic, however. Anyone who sets high standards for themselves and is driven to succeed will make it in sales if they also enjoy and understand people. This doesn't mean they need to slap the backs and shake the hands of everyone in a room they enter. It means they enjoy helping people make a buying decision while knowing that the decision will benefit both sides.

Wherever I go and whatever I'm doing, I look forward to meeting people. I want to learn about them, and I take a serious interest in things they say and do. I learn about people by asking questions, something that those who know me well often comment about. It's because I have always had a thirst for learning and a curiosity about facts and people.

3. They spend more time listening than talking.

I was often reminded as a child that we humans were born with two ears but just one mouth. The implication was obvious: we are more suited to listening than to talking. Like all clichés, this one happens to be true. Successful selling isn't about drowning a customer in facts and figures. It's about asking questions and listening carefully, not just to what is being said but also *how* it is being said and what is *not* being said. Tone and delivery can reveal much about whatever the speaker is trying to express in words. And body language can communicate a world of meaning without a word being spoken, or in spite of a word that may have an entirely different meaning from whatever the speaker intended. Failure to listen and watch carefully when someone is speaking risks missing the heart of the message the person is trying to convey.

4. They make the connection between selling skills and life.

Among the lines of everything I reveal in this book is this message: *the most important thing you will ever sell is yourself.* The same skills valued in selling are equally valued in almost every other aspect of your life.

Have you heard this before? You may hear it again in this book. It sums up my overall message, and it represents much of my ability to get the most out of life. Everything we do is evaluated according to the same principles applied to selling. Our appearance, our manner, our values, our skills—they all represent measures that determine the success of salespeople, and the same qualities can be applied when dealing with everyone who is important in our lives.

Whether choosing a life partner, raising our children, seeking a job, running for political office, or performing a hundred other actions, we must persuade others to see *our* point of view, follow *our* lead, and value *our* abilities.

Most of the decisions we make in life are determined more by our heart than by our brain. Intelligence is wonderful and plays an essential role in the decisions we make, but when it comes to decisions that affect us personally—or, if you prefer, subjectively rather than objectively—*emotion trumps intellect.*

Nothing illustrates this better than the process of reaching a buying decision. Buyers will spend hours studying the details of a car, a washer and dryer, a video system, even a jet aircraft. They will fill their heads with as much data as they can gather and use computer apps to compare alternatives, all in pursuit of making the best choice. But in the end it won't be their mind alone making the decision; it will include their heart's response as well. And more often than not, the heart will overwhelm the brain. If the brain is stymied—if the intellectual approach cannot arrive at a clear decision—the emotional factor will always tip the scales. Always.

Perhaps the most important point I can make about the process of selling is to explain that all of us are ruled by both our brains and our hearts—and not always equally. We are driven by intellect and emotion, and to forget or eliminate the impact of emotion—what our hearts tell us we want—blinds us not only to the secret of successful selling but also to our ability to get as much enjoyment from our lives as possible.

I mean, even sharks have emotional centers.

Including the ones on television.

SEVEN

Inside the Shark Tank

Shark Tank has won more than its share of industry awards, including two prime-time Emmys, two Critics' Choice Awards, a Television Critics Association Award, and umpteen nominations from every major awards show in the industry. Several reasons account for its success since its premiere show in August 2009, and one of them is the enormous amount of behind-the-scenes energy invested in each episode. Viewers have little or no idea what's involved, which is as it should be—the mark of true professionals is their ability to conceal all the hard work and stress needed to crank out a quality product. The magic of the show grows not out of the actions of we Sharks and the deals we might haggle over. It's fashioned by the producers, directors, analysts, and other people behind the scenes who select the pitches and stage them for maximum impact on us and on the viewers.

Start with some numbers. Each season between 40,000 and 50,000 people either apply for an audition on *Shark Tank* or are invited to submit information on their business venture for consideration. Many applications are rejected immediately based on the quality of the submission. Others move through a multistage selection process before being invited to make an in-person pitch to the producers. Meanwhile, *Shark Tank* analysts scout business media and business trade shows in search of companies with an unusual product or service and an apparent need for investment funds. Out of those thousands of people and their business dreams who apply or are selected for consideration, about 225 are invited to make their pitch. These are further winnowed down until about 150 appear on air each season.

Why don't the others appear on your TV screen? To put it bluntly, they're boring. They may be wonderful people, salt of the earth, and even succeed in making a deal with us, but if in the opinion of the producers they fail to seize your interest, they won't make it into your home via your television screen. You can fix many things in television and movies, but you can't fix boring. If you are fat, thin, bald, wrinkled, or almost any other physical situation that doesn't play well to audiences, it can be corrected. But if you are boring, you are stuck with it, and Hollywood will move on without you.

I'm not suggesting that anyone hoping for an appearance on *Shark Tank* show up in a weird or scanty costume, or wear a funny hat and do a silly dance. That's not what they need. They need to tell an interesting story in an exciting manner. The entertainment industry calls this giving value to the viewer, and that's a good term. We invest money in the dreams of the pitchers on *Shark Tank*. Viewers invest an hour of their lives in watching the show, and they deserve something of value in return. Boring has little or no value anywhere.

Shark Tank producers look for businesses and people that they know will make great TV, and the most important part of this mix, by far, is the people and their situations. Entertainment of all kinds is based on those two elements, reality show or not.

The business aspect is secondary. You don't win two Emmys and numerous other awards because you have a great business show on television. You win those awards because you have an entertaining show whose subject matter is business.

That's what is missing among the knockoff shows that have tried to cash in on the success of *Shark Tank*. The people behind these productions say, "Hey, let's make a business show that will attract millions of viewers like *Shark Tank*." That's their first mistake. *Shark Tank* is not a business show; it's a reality TV drama dealing with high-stakes interactions between people, and the topic happens to be business.

Dramatic situations make great television, and great television, when it occurs, is nothing less than magic. It's like great businesses. Both have an element of magic in them, and our producers and crew create magic over and over every week we're on the air. What you cannot do in making magic or a great business is write a can't-miss formula to be handed out for other people to duplicate the magic. It just doesn't happen that way. The only way to explain how *Shark Tank* producers achieve magic is to say they know it when they see it. That's their gift—the talent they use to find magic—and they always begin with people and personalities.

Reality TV is character-driven, not idea- or situation-driven. You can build a show around a fascinating character, but good luck building success around a product or a business. Nothing proves this better than the success of the Kardashians. The show is all about them and what they are—outlandish, self-centered, opinionated, and a lot of other descriptions, few of them flattering. You don't have to like the Kardashians to follow their adventures. You just have to be sufficiently fascinated by them.

We want to be fascinated by the people who appear on *Shark*

Tank looking for investment funding. Anyone who comes into the studio brimming with high energy, confidence, and determination changes the tone of the room immediately. We become excited, we begin asking questions, we give and receive feedback, and somewhere along the line we become interested in the business side of their story. That's what pulls viewers back to the show week after week. They know us and the way we respond to different situations. It's the unique and surprising personalities of the pitchers, and the chemistry that erupts between them and us, that make great television.

Does this sound simple? It's not, and the statistics prove it.

Every year the TV networks "green light" about a hundred shows, meaning they get approved for development. Out of these about fifteen are actually produced—scripts are written, characters or participants are cast, studios are booked and decorated, and an actual episode is ready for viewing. Viewers never see most of these produced shows because only about three are aired and few of these survive their first season.

The magic behind the show's success starts with the selection of pitchers and relies on many things other than the appeal of the pitchers themselves. Once they have appeared and the episode has been recorded, the next most important bit of magic is the editing. Viewers at home watch each pitch spin out, from start to finish, over about seven or eight minutes. Things move along quickly—the pitchers do their spiel, the Sharks push for details and either make an offer or bow out, and it all ends with either a handshake or a slow walk by the pitchers out of the studio.

That's what the audience sees, but it's not all that happens. The average encounter with pitchers lasts a full hour—sixty minutes of back-and-forth chatter, bickering, cajoling, and deciding. Even the shortest encounter took thirty-five minutes. The longest was two and a half hours—longer than a Hollywood feature film. Being able to reduce these minimarathons to the length of a coffee break while keeping the story line together is another measure of magic that contributes to the show's popularity.

Finally, there's a side to the magic element of the show that says something about the greatness of America. When you set aside the cameras and the promotion and the glitz and Emmys, the show is really about us—meaning you and me and every American who harbors a dream. Some of us have achieved that dream, or enough of it that we have satisfied much of our ambition. Others are working at theirs, and knowing the odds against them appearing on the show, let alone walking away with the investment funds they were seeking, they make the effort and keep their dreams alive.

The impact this has on me and the other Sharks is enormous. We may sit there weighing the pros and cons of the pitches we hear and deciding to walk away without handing over a penny if we choose. We all enjoy our success, both the emotional satisfaction it brings us and the material benefits we have earned. We don't have to wake up every morning worrying if we will make the rent payment that day, and we don't have to dream about what it's like to drive a Ferrari or slip into a sable coat because one (or more) is in our garage or closet. So you may expect that a large part of us wants everything to be constant and unchanging. We don't have to keep that sales curve rising like a hockey stick, right?

Wrong. We do. One of the most popular principles to be followed by independent businesspeople is to accept that there is no constant, no point at which you say, "I guess I can back off the throttle and coast for a while." Well, you can't. In business you either grow fast or die slowly.

The people who make the cut and appear in front of us to pitch their offer, baring their souls (or at least their dreams) to us, are not interested in coasting. We were once *them,* and they want to be *us,* and witnessing their drive to succeed motivates me and the other Sharks.

Not all of them will succeed, of course. Life doesn't work that way. But the show demonstrates that you can be somebody in this country without being an athlete or a movie star. Nobody else in the world has the same opportunity to crave success against overwhelming odds as Americans. The belief that you can make anything you want of your life is so classically American that it defines the country.

My participation on *Shark Tank* has opened my eyes to another side to that story, and it's all about second chances and transformations. No people in the world love a comeback story more than Americans, and it doesn't have to be related to sports. An untold number of businesses, and the people who created them, have made it onto *Shark Tank* having almost touched success at one point, only to see it slip from their grasp, often due to bad luck. They're down but not out, and if we encounter these people, recognize their potential, and see a chance to help both of us, we tend to jump aboard.

All of us on the show have favorite stories that illustrate this approach. Mine involves a great husband-and-wife team, Hanna and Mark Lim. The parents of young children, they had developed a child's drinking cup that was far superior to existing designs. Their Lollacup made it much easier for a child to drink liquids without spilling them and much easier for parents to clean all of its parts. Hanna and Mark went a step further by insisting that their products be manufactured in the United States or Germany to ensure that they were free of materials deemed harmful to children.

Their company began growing steadily until Hanna became seriously ill. It took a year for her to fully recover and resume building the firm, but sales and production had slipped badly in that time—so badly that some people would have cut their losses and looked for steady employment elsewhere. Mark Cuban and I both recognized the brilliant design and superb execution of their product, along with Hanna and Mark's determination. That's what sold us on them. With the funds we invested in the company, the Lims grew from assembling the products part-time in their garage to setting up a full assembly line in a modern warehouse. They also expanded their dealer network from about fifty stores doing $40,000 worth of sales to nationwide distribution achieving millions of dollars in sales.

Most people believe we Sharks go through all those hours of listening to pitches and making investment decisions strictly for the profit we hope to earn. I would be a fool to say that's not correct. But I would also be wrong to say that it's the only thing that motivates us.

Stories like the Lims' reinforce our belief in the opportunity to succeed that distinguishes America. It reminds viewers of just how fortunate they are to be here, and perhaps will inspire more than a handful to take advantage of their good fortune.

That sounds like flag waving, I know. But I needed to make my point.

There have been times, however, when the show has revealed another aspect of American life, the one based on unlimited free speech between people who disagree. Or, in this case, Sharks.

EIGHT

Shark Bites

I'm the first to credit the producers, directors, editors, and other crew members for the remarkable success of *Shark Tank* over the years. With the Emmys and other awards the show has earned, it's easy to assume that it was a guaranteed hit from the beginning. Nothing in life is guaranteed, least of all a network TV show, and *Shark Tank* struggled over the first season or two until we all had a handle on what worked, what didn't work, and what was needed to make the show work better.

Earlier I mentioned the critical importance of finding pitchers whose personality and backstory were intriguing or inspiring or unique—anything but boring. Put a character in front of us who holds our attention on them and freezes the viewers' eyes on their TV screens, and we have a winning segment of a good show.

Obviously, that's only half the story. The other half consists of netting the right kind of Shark to hear their tale and decide either to bite or drift away. For the show's success, one of the most important qualities—some people may argue that it's the *only* important quality—is our focus on the potential return from our investment. In other words, to quote Kevin O'Leary, perhaps the most fearsome Shark of all, *we want to make MONEY!!!* That's Kevin's brand. The rest of us share similar ambitions. We just have a different way of going about it. And it's these differences—our contrasting brands, if you will—that make the show work so well.

(This is not entirely true, as I explained in the previous chapter. Our emotional response to pitchers can color the decision of whether to buy in or get out. Emotion can influence the decision, but it cannot be the only factor in being in or out of a deal. At times, I suspect it plays no role at all in any of Kevin's decisions, but I'm ready to have him prove me wrong.)

Every show business production—and I repeat that *Shark Tank* is as much *show* as it is *business*—needs a recurring cast of characters, and the chemistry between them accounts for the show's overall appeal. Four of us Sharks—Barbara, Daymond, Kevin, and I—have been part of the show from the beginning. It took a while to bring Mark Cuban aboard. His openly aggressive attitude, along with Kevin's *"Show me the money!"* demands, served as a balance with the comparatively "nice" personalities of Barbara (or Lori), Daymond, and me. It was all about chemistry. Five Marks or Kevins on the show would be abrasive, and five "nice" panelists like Barbara/Lori, Daymond, and me would risk being (*shudder*) boring.

The truth is, none of us Sharks is consistently "nice" to each other. There are times when we honestly do not like each other, and we hold nothing back. That's what makes it a true reality show. Each caustic comment you hear and each roll of the eyes you see on the show is impulsive and real. No one on the show tells us what to do, how to act, or what to say. Everything is close to the surface, including our feelings. The only thing we may be mindful of is the personal brand each of us has established over the years. They are unique to us—on *Shark Tank,* at least—and they go a long way toward building the viewer loyalty we enjoy.

The concept of people being branded like packaged goods is new to some people and insulting to many. "I am not a can of soda," they may say, and they are correct. No one, including me, wants to be packaged and presented like goods displayed on a shelf, although a few Hollywood stars might admit that their studios and PR handlers come close to that approach. Personal branding should focus on unique personal aspects that individuals shape to their advantage.

Compare Mark Cuban, for example, with Kevin O'Leary. Both are aggressive; unyielding; and, to many people, terrifying to face. But they are different people in their approach to business. Kevin spends more time building his brand than anyone I know, and it's based on greed and intimidation. Along with billing himself as "Mr. Wonderful," his supposed total focus is on improving his cash position every day, over and over. He once declared that he considers every dollar he owns a soldier, and each morning he sends his millions of "soldiers" out into the world to seize prisoners—dollar bills—and bring them home by sundown.

Mark loves wealth every bit as much as Kevin, but his view is not skewed toward building his immediate cash position. He and I are interested in building viable companies that will grow and prosper in the future, providing employment and security for hundreds of employees and eventually a substantial return for us as investors. If you think of this difference between us when you watch a *Shark Tank* episode, it will explain how Mark, Kevin, and I evaluate the deals offered us by the pitchers. We have different goals, different ways of dealing with people, and different attitudes toward business generally. The differences define our personal brands.

Daymond John is as conscious of branding as the rest of us, but his focus is on his business more than his personal brand. The man walks, talks, and constantly sells FUBU, his brand of urban clothing. Good branding, Daymond preaches, means that people know about your product—what is does, how it looks, what it stands for, and how much it costs—before they encounter it. The same measure, Daymond says, works for people as well. The real secret of personal branding success, according to Daymond, is being able to describe yourself in six words or less. When I asked what he thought my brand might be, Daymond suggested *Internet security provider who has fun.*

Hey, I can live with that.

Branding aside, the emotional factor I referred to in the previous chapter is in play on *Shark Tank* as much as in everyday selling situations. And once again the feelings are always close to the surface.

Sometimes the emotions we share are dark and dismissive. Sometimes they're bright and complimentary. It depends on what we're being sold, how well the seller is doing, and how we Sharks feel toward each other at the time. One thing that often drives us mad is when the person looking to make a deal with us cannot provide sales or profit figures for the business they want us to buy into. How can someone ask for our money when they can't tell us how much money they're making from whatever it is they want us to invest in? Yet we may cut them some slack and even offer words of encouragement if not stacks of money.

We may also, however, hammer someone who fails just as

much in providing the data we need. We coddle one and condemn the other. Why? For two reasons. The first may be the obvious potential of the idea being pitched to us. We may see, in far sharper focus, the future possibilities of the deal, and after performing our due diligence be prepared to work with them. The other is—or can be—an emotional connection they made with us in the opening moments of their pitch. It doesn't mean we'll hand over our money more easily or generously. But it can affect our attitude toward both the pitcher and the deal.

As cold and hard-hearted as we Sharks may be when making an investment decision, we can—and do—respond to a positive emotional link between us and whoever is looking for our money to fund their company. Make that connection, and we Sharks will be on your side, giving you a chance to finish your pitch and treating you perhaps a little more gently than we think you deserve. Miss it, and we'll start pointing to the door.

The emotional aspect of *Shark Tank* represents a key appeal of the show. And, by the way, all of it is sincere. None of us is an actor. We're on the show because we are businesspeople first. That's our occupation and our identity. We also happen to be competitive and, when needed, stubborn and outspoken.

That's the show's total premise: five successful businesspeople, each with a different background and focus, searching for ways to make money by competing against the others. And yes, we're talking real money here—*our* real money. When a deal is done and the necessary due diligence is completed, we hand over the cash as promised. None of us, in case it needs to be said, accumulated our wealth by tossing money around carelessly. We value every dollar we own, and we take care before we hand it over to someone we met in the studio a few minutes earlier. The pitchers are there offering us an opportunity to make money from a serious business proposition. They did not show up with the goal of convincing us they're nice folks who need a helping hand.

It's supposed to work that way. When it doesn't . . . well, things can run off the rails and lead to the kind of outburst that occurred between Lori Grenier and me that has become infamous. I told Lori her actions had "pissed me off," angry words were exchanged between all of us, Mark Cuban and Kevin O'Leary followed me out of the studio trailing wisps of smoke, and none of it was staged. It was all very real, driven by anger and serious disagreement.

How did it happen?

Remember that it takes an hour, on average, to complete a pitch on *Shark Tank,* and can last as long as two and a half hours. That's a long time for anyone to sit in one place, even if they hope to make a profit somewhere down the road. But that's what we do.

Just to make it more demanding on our composure, we record an entire season of *Shark Tank* over seventeen days, never spending more than three days in a row in the studio. Out of those seventeen days the producers aim to craft thirty-four episodes that will run through the season. It's necessary to compress an entire season's production into such a short time because we all run companies doing hundreds of millions of dollars' worth of business, and the time we can spare away from them is scarce.

Three days don't represent just the maximum number of days we can stay away from our businesses; it's the maximum number of days we can do our jobs as Sharks and still remain functional. Not to mention amiable and courteous with each other. I call it our shelf life: after three days we get stale. Or musty. Or sour. Especially sour.

These are long twelve-hour days. We're at the studio between six and seven in the morning, basically locked inside until six or seven at night. ABC-TV and the producers treat us well, but we're all strong personalities, and spending that much time in one place can make us antsy. Especially by the third day.

I've tracked the changes that occur to us over those three-day sessions. The first day is generally a good one. We reacquaint ourselves with each other and get a buzz from routine preparations, trading gossip, catching up on each other's careers, and talking with crew members in the studio. While doing this we're also trying to put whatever was going on in our business or personal lives out of our minds. When the lights and cameras are on we need to pay exclusive attention to whatever unfolds on the set. Good businesspeople know how to adapt to whatever situation they find themselves in, and we manage to do it, but we need to work at it.

None of us, as I said, is an actor. Still, we have those brands to think of and our own personalities to deal with. The things we do and say on the first day of shooting are carved a little more sharply than later. Or maybe we're just hamming it up together. For the first few hours of day one Kevin snarls a little more, Mark is pushier, Lori sharpens her TV smarts, Barbara plays her strict den mother role with greater relish, and Daymond seems to rise even farther above it all. I tend to smile more easily, finding it all entertaining and refreshing. Later on that first day we begin settling down to our routines.

Day two is inevitably the best. Those twelve-hour studio sessions have become our reality, and nothing intrudes on our assessment of the pitches (and the people making them).

Day three may begin well, but as the hours pass, it becomes difficult to keep our minds off whatever we hope or fear is happening back at the office. It also becomes trickier to overlook little annoyances that were easy to shrug off a day or two earlier, when they might have earned a smile or a joke tossed between us for a laugh. Now they begin to grate at us.

Through it all, we see ourselves as a family of sorts. A dysfunctional family at times, but a family nevertheless. Like many families, each member's emotions are near the surface, and things can flare up with a suddenness and a fury that would be shocking to outsiders. We may feel cold, hungry, frustrated, and concerned about far-off personal or business crises. If enough of us share these feelings, we are collectively primed to explode with a flash of sarcasm or a blast of anger.

How do the producers react to these outbreaks of anger and frustration? They love 'em. They even have a name for them: *Shark bites.*

Which brings me back to Lori and me.

Remember my earlier comment that *Shark Tank* is a place for business deals, not hand-outs? I'm not opposed to helping people in need. Nor is anyone else on the show. All of us make charitable contributions to whatever organizations we choose. What we give, how much we give, and who we give it to are our business, and none of it has anything to do with investing in a business. Any business. We all subscribe to this premise. At least we did until first Lori and then Daymond broke the custom.

We were being pitched by a bright and pleasant young man named Christopher Gray, who had developed an app to locate available college scholarships for qualified students. He explained that as much as $100 million in scholarships goes unclaimed each year because deserving students were not aware of the existence of the scholarships.

Gray's app, which he named Scholly, addressed this need. Scholly tapped all the scholarships available to students across the

United States. Users of the program inserted personal information about themselves, and the program alerted them to the scholarships they appeared qualified to claim. Gray, the son of a single mother, claimed he had earned $1.3 million in scholarships for himself and that Scholly, priced at 99 cents, had already registered more than 90,000 sales. He was asking for a $40,000 injection of cash in exchange for 15 percent of his company.

I was impressed. So were Mark and Kevin. But the three of us had questions. We wanted to know how he would grow the company over time and how he planned to update his database of tens of thousands of scholarships year by year. These were legitimate issues, but we barely had time to ask a couple of questions before Lori blurted out, "I don't know how we're going to monetize it, but I want to shake your hand and say 'deal.'"

When I questioned Lori's premature move without fully understanding his company's operations and prospects, all she could say was that she believed in Gray and in his business model.

"How can you believe in it," I asked her, "when you haven't asked him anything about the business?"

That's when Daymond offered to share the $40,000 cash injection with Lori, and the deal was done. Gray left the studio with a wide smile on his face, having been offered everything he had requested without answering any serious questions.

I was upset over Lori and Daymond's move, and it had nothing to do with them making a deal before I had a chance to jump in. My disagreement was over their decision to make a commitment without having even a grasp of important facts. Lori's explanation to me was that she wanted to help America and make the world a better place. This had nothing to do with the quality of the investment. I interpreted her comments to mean she and Daymond had offered Gray a handout.

"You know," I said, and I could feel the fire rising within me, "when my family was poor, I hated it when people wanted to give us a break because they felt sorry for us." I added that my father, a proud man, had rejected every offer of charity ever offered to him. "This is the *Shark Tank*," I reminded her, "not the charity tank."

Kevin and Mark had been silent to this point, but Kevin noted that he had not been allowed to make an offer because Lori "had to force $40,000 down Gray's throat like a goose for pâté." Mark shared the same opinion, and when Lori made another excuse for acting hastily, I momentarily lost it. "You're really pissing me off right now," I said. As I stood to walk out of the studio, I explained that I was not going to comment further because as a child I had been advised not to say anything about someone if I couldn't say anything nice about them. Mark and Kevin followed me.

This shook up a lot of viewers. Some were shocked but others, I suspect, loved it because it was both real and unexpected. *Real*—they sensed our serious disagreement and frustration with the way Lori and Daymond handled things. They knew emotions were running deep and that we were all being totally, even brutally, honest with each other.

None of this had any long-term effect on the relationship between us. As I indicated earlier, we really are like a family whose members are comfortable expressing themselves without holding anything back.

What about Christopher Gray and his Scholly program?

After leaving the studio, Gray confirmed the concerns that Kevin, Mark, and I had wanted to make with Lori and Daymond. "I'm really happy to find two Sharks," he said, "who care more about what Scholly's going to do for the public than about the bottom line." In other words, the quality of the investment he wanted from us wasn't important; only the effect that he hoped to make on needy college students mattered. That's fine for a charity, but it had nothing to do with good investment practices, and everything to do offering a handout.

I make investments and charitable contributions every year. In both cases I look into the things my money is expected to do, and how it will benefit everyone involved. I keep my investments and my charitable contributions separate, along with my expectations for each. I suggest everyone do that, Shark or not.

By the way, I understand that Scholly is doing well, and I assume that Lori's and Daymond's investment is paying off for them.

Good for them.

But my position still stands: investments are one thing, charity is something else, and making one on the basis of the other is foolish.

NINE

The World Owes You Nothing—Except Opportunity

I missed out on a lot of things when growing up. I didn't have nice clothes or the latest toys, I didn't attend concerts or ball games, and I didn't go to summer camp or on family vacations. Most of the things that other kids bragged about enjoying were alien to me.

Did it bother me to miss these things? Sure it did. And I was bothered as well by my parents. To be blunt, they embarrassed me, which I hate to admit. My mom and dad were awkward around other people. They didn't wear cool clothes, and they spoke in funny accents, and I hated it. Maybe you have to be an immigrant kid wanting to "fit in" with friends to understand how I felt.

One day I was walking home from school with a friend when I noticed an odd-looking man coming toward us. He was unshaven and wearing old clothes, with a cigarette dangling out of his mouth. As we passed he said hi to me. "Is that your dad?" my friend asked, and I told him no, it was some old guy from the neighborhood. I was embarrassed by my father's appearance, but I was even more embarrassed about denying that he was my dad. My father may not have looked the way I wanted him to, but he was a hardworking and basically honest man who had sacrificed much to provide my mother and me with a better life than we had in Yugoslavia. He did not deserve my rejection of him that way.

Years later, when my son was attending university, I discovered he was denying to his friends that I was his father, just as I had with my dad. My son's reason was very different from mine. I had lied because my father embarrassed me; he just wanted his friends to like him for himself and not because of his father, who often appeared on television and in magazines. You might say he was doing it for the right reason, but the irony of the situation stung anyway.

I also realized that both situations demonstrated a fact that we all need to acknowledge and follow: *no one owes you anything in life.*

When I was a schoolboy I believed that my father owed it to me to be a well-dressed, English-speaking, middle-class dad like my friends' fathers. He didn't, of course. He gave me a chance to set my life goals and enjoy the freedom to reach them. That's all I had a right to expect.

My son understood this from an early age. He did not want to be popular with friends solely because his father was a well-known businessman who appeared regularly on network television. He wanted to be accepted for who he was and the things he achieved on his own. No one, including me, owed him popularity and success, and he refused to exploit whatever advantage came with having my last name. I understand and respect him so much for that decision.

The idea that it's up to you and no one else to make whatever you want of your life is hardly new. If your grandparents lived through war, economic depression, and political upheaval of the past century, they don't need to be reminded of the wisdom of that advice. They probably lived it every day, and their lives were molded by the experience.

Whenever I learn of a young person who was born into a famous and wealthy family, and who winds up in serious trouble over and over again, I hear many people say with annoyance, "Why can't he/she just smarten up?"

My reaction is somewhat different. I think, "Too bad nobody ever told them that the world doesn't owe them a thing."

If there's a bank account of life, the balance is empty when you are born. Nobody made a deposit for you. Nothing in your account is earning interest. And anything you deposit in the account must be earned by you alone. I'm not referring to money and material things. I'm talking about the aspects of life that determine your happiness and self-satisfaction. You don't win it, and you don't inherit it. You work for it.

No one else is living your life for you. No one can. All of us, if we are fortunate, are in control of our own lives. We may not always be responsible for what happens to us, but we are responsible for our own reaction to it and how we let it affect us.

Here's another thought that may not have occurred to you: *no one has to love and respect you, and you should never expect that they will on their own.* Those who honestly love you recognize something about you that gives them pleasure. That's where love and respect begin.

Consider the lesson in that thought: when you can identify that quality, you can use it to create stronger and deeper love from others. People don't like you out of duty. They like you because something about you, some element in your personality, makes *them* feel happy to be around *you*. They don't owe you their love and respect. You need to earn it.

Instead of believing that the world owes you something, shift your view to this idea:

The only person who owes you anything is yourself.

You owe it to yourself to be the best person you can be, someone others are attracted to for the reasons I mentioned above. Those qualities can provide you with all the important things you want from life—happiness, love, and respect—to the same degree that you provide them to others. One more time: *no one gives these things to you; you earn them.* When things go wrong in your life, often the place to find the root cause is by looking in a mirror.

The best route to success, in my opinion, is to view the dark side of reality not as something to be overcome or feared, but to accept and apply. I'm all for dreaming about things I might achieve. Dreams are the basis of creativity, and I don't want to stop imagining things I might accomplish, because it leads to creating new ideas to be explored and developed. I just refuse to live my entire life in my dreams, and so should you.

Accepting that the world owes you nothing can be a great motivator. It teaches you that the way to get something from someone else is by entering their world—discovering how *they* think, what *they* believe is important, and what *their* wants and needs are. Can you think of three things more valuable to someone making a career as a salesperson? Or, for that matter, someone looking for a friend or life partner?

Neither can I.

*   *   *

The world owes you only one thing: *opportunity.*

That's it. That's all.

This opportunity exists at its highest and most favorable level in North America. I say that knowing that many people find themselves trapped behind barriers that make it difficult to realize their dreams. Those barriers are familiar. They include race, education, economic level, and gender, and they still exist in America but they are not entirely insurmountable. Daymond John, an African American raised by a single mother in Queens, and Barbara Corcoran, a white woman waiting tables in a diner, are proof of that. Are they exceptions? Yes, they are. They are also exceptional people because they overcame barriers that millions of Americans believe bar them from success.

Many of us face the same kinds of barriers, and we have to work harder to reach the same level as others who avoided them at birth. The color of your skin, your gender, your location, and a dozen other things over which you have no control can trip you up, but only if you let them. They justify the universal truth that life is basically unfair. Damn right it is. Success can be hard to achieve but it is not always impossible, even though it can appear that way. One of the great joys of my life has been to achieve the impossible while others stand around muttering that it cannot be done.

Anyone who knew me as a kid who could speak maybe a dozen words of English when he left Croatia might have assumed my most likely career would involve sweeping factory floors like my father. Well, they were wrong. If you face the same kind of obstacles that threatened to block the ambitions of Daymond, Barbara, and me, you can prove skeptics wrong as well.

You will have to accept some risks to do it, but that's the nature of life. Nothing worthwhile is achieved without risk, from crossing the street to launching a career in sales . . . or starting your own company.

Most of the serious risks we face in life exist not because we *want* to take them, but because we *need* to take them. I didn't start my first company so I could make enough money to buy a Ferrari or two. I started it because I had been fired from my previous job and needed to pay the bills. I took the risk of applying my sales ability and becoming an entrepreneur to escape the certainty of being broke and homeless. The choice was easy. Risks are an inevitable part of life. Success lies in taking measured risks, and avoiding the big risks that can destroy your dreams of success.

Reaping the rewards of being a successful salesperson involves a level of risk similar to that of choosing to launch your own company. For example, you may have to forget about the security of a guaranteed salary or a guaranteed anything where your income is concerned. Most of the money that top salespeople take home is earned from commissions on the sales they make, and that's fine with them. They accept the rule of the marketplace (and maybe of life in general): *the greater the risk, the greater the potential reward.*

Choosing a career in sales also means accepting another kind of risk. Many jobs in the business world make it easy to disguise mediocre performance, because it is difficult to accurately measure how well each employee is doing his or her job. Managers use performance reviews, peer assessments, and various other ways to rate employees, but when the primary responsibility involves moving papers around, where's the measure? I'm not suggesting these jobs are unimportant; I'm just pointing out how gray the picture can be when trying to decide how well some jobs are being done. Most job performance ratings are basically guesswork.

Selling is different. When it comes to evaluating the work of a salesperson, it all comes down to measuring performance against sales quota.

> You made your quota this month? That's nice; keep up the
>   good work.
> You exceeded your quota this month? That's terrific; here's
>   a pat on the back, and maybe a bonus.
> You missed your quota again this month? Maybe it's time
>   for a little chat.

So choosing a career in sales means accepting the fact that your success will be based on hard, measurable data. Make your sales quota each month, and your job is safe. Miss your quota too often, and you're history. That's the risk good salespeople and entrepreneurs accept. And they tend to thrive on it.

Is all that risk worth it? Yes, if you understand the difference between good risks and bad risks.

Taking good risks helps me build my company. Good risks are based on careful research, proper planning, and expecting a potential reward that exceeds any losses if things don't work out. Bad risks are often impulsively taken and with a potentially disastrous downside, making them more of a gamble than a reasonable decision. Taking bad risks could mean the death of my company. I avoid bad risks because death is almost always fatal.

If you're more interested in coasting through a risk-free job than aiming for a level of success that potentially can make you wealthy, selling isn't for you. But if the idea of a career where recognition and reward are directly linked to the amount of hard work you do sounds appealing, you're probably in the right place. And if you want to do all of this with time for diversions like a game of golf or hanging out with family or friends now and then, it could get even better.

Is that latter benefit a contradiction? No; it's just the reality of being a good salesperson.

Selling is one of the few careers available where the number of hours you work are not always related to the amount of money you earn. Meeting your sales quota every month is like getting the rent paid—you know how much money you made, and it's there for you. So if you like, you can take an afternoon off and go shopping or just take a long walk in the park. And if you like the idea of being an entrepreneur but want time for family, friends, and hobbies, a sales career in a large company may be the only way to do both.

All you need to get started is the ambition to succeed and the passion to discover and do what you enjoy doing most. Many of us have the ambition. And everyone who dreams of reaching some higher level of success in life has a reservoir of passion waiting to be tapped. Passion can turn a warm, fuzzy dream into a satisfying reality. And passion to launch and maintain a satisfying career can be a positive force that urges us to improve our lot in life, creating comfort and security for our families and ourselves.

But it is effective only when we recognize that cold, hard truth from several pages ago—the one that dictates no one should expect the world owes them something.

Because it doesn't.

TEN

How Do You Know What You're Good At?

I once read a magazine interview with a musician on his eighty-fifth birthday. He was a trumpet player and had earned his living playing jazz since he was a teenager. A gentle soul with a warm sense of humor, he was always in demand to play with local jazz and dance bands.

When the interviewer asked the trumpet player what had made him such a good musician, the man looked confused. Then he shrugged, smiled, and said, "It's not that I was such a good musician. It's just that I was so lousy at everything else."

I suspect many people follow their careers in a similar fashion. They wander here and there, not sure of what to do with their lives until they find something they seem able to do well enough to earn a living. In contrast, others fix on their careers early and do whatever it takes to make it happen. They become doctors, lawyers, engineers, or members of some other profession, intent on success from their first day in college. Instead of wandering, they follow a fixed line on their way to wherever they want to be. Kym Johnson is one of those people. She started dancing when she was three years old and went down the path to success as a professional dancer with fury and energy until she reached her goal of becoming a professional dancer.

The difference between people like Kym and others is the passion I spoke about earlier. Those with passion to succeed follow their dream with enthusiasm and purpose. Those without similar passion find humdrum jobs that fail to fulfill them.

Incidentally, I believe the trumpet player was joking. He knew from an early age that his passion was music, and he pursued it. He did not become the most famous trumpet player in the world, but that wasn't his goal. His goal, I suspect, was to play the kind of music he enjoyed as often as possible, and be paid for it. In that sense he was successful all through a long and fulfilling life. He had satisfied his passion.

Where is your passion to succeed centered? And where can you find a formula for success?

The first question is yours to answer. The second question is mine to handle, and here it is:

No one has a foolproof formula for success. It doesn't exist. The best I can do is offer a three-step plan that puts the odds in your favor.

Begin by identifying something you are good at. It should be a talent or an ability that comes naturally to you, and that you enjoy doing. If you enjoy doing it enough—if, in a moment of total honesty, you can say that you would do it whether you were paid to or not—you have probably found your passion.

Next, work until you become good at it. Then, when you are good, keep working until you become great at it. And when you achieve greatness, never stop trying to get even better.

Finally, forget your weaknesses and focus on your strengths. The part of your passion that is easiest to deliver is the part you need to work at most. If you are a golfer and your drives are spectacular but your putting is weak, concentrate on improving your drives. If you are a painter and your depictions of hills and valleys are far better than your portraits, work on your landscapes.

At first this sounds contradictory to a lot of popular advice. "Be well rounded," you may read in self-help books and hear spouted by televised career counselors. "Work on your weaknesses until they are as good as your strong points."

But here's the problem:

No matter how hard you work on your weak points, you are unlikely to ever make them better or even as good as the things that come naturally to you. Your natural talents won't improve because you're spending all that time and energy on that weak spot. Instead of becoming "well rounded," you will become merely mediocre. And guess what? The world does not reward mediocrity. It rewards greatness and exceptional results.

Greatness almost always lies not in the broad picture but in the narrow window, the place where someone can stand head and shoulders above others. Identify that passion, whatever it may be—sweeping factory floors, developing a computer code, dancing a cha-cha, or racing a car around a racetrack—and aim to be the very best at it. The world is a competitive place, and somewhere there is someone determined to kick your butt. The most successful people I know are the ones who love to win. If you are not intent at winning in whatever arena you choose for your life, or you are simply uncomfortable about competition of any kind, you are not likely to get ahead in whatever endeavor you choose.

Back to the part about identifying your passion.

This step demands total honesty on your part, because you are not just looking for something you *want* to do; you are also searching for something you are *able* to do. You may dream of becoming a top fashion designer or bush pilot or some other enticing occupation. Dreams are wonderful things, and everyone should feel free to imagine themselves achieving enormous success in whatever they wish to do. But remember my caution earlier in this book. Believing you can become whoever and whatever you choose to be is the right attitude; choosing to do it despite real and unavoidable handicaps that can overwhelm you is a mistake.

You may have been spellbound as a child when watching competitive ice skaters at the Olympics. It might even have inspired you to dream of doing spins and triple axels at the Olympics, with all the lights and cameras upon you and the audience applauding every leap. It's a wonderful dream and one that is worth striving to achieve . . . until the first time you strap on a pair of ice skates and experience the reality of it all. Should you try anyway? Of course you should, if your passion is powerful enough. And if you accept the vast difference between what can be imagined and what can realistically be achieved.

There is also the age factor. To everything, we are reminded, there is a season, and if your dream involves doing something out of season—tackling it too late in life—you need to be honest with yourself. This kind of honesty can be painful, as is the advice that often goes along with it. In the end, painful honesty is more important than sweet self-delusion.

I had a friend who, in her late teens, decided on a career in ballet. She treasured the dream of performing onstage, where she just knew she would be a picture of grace and beauty. Ballerinas, in her opinion, represented the ultimate in elegance and artistic expression. They also, I gently reminded her, begin training as very young children. Then, even more gently, I wondered if her height and body shape were ideal for ballet.

Not surprisingly, she did not appreciate my observations. Becoming a ballerina was her goal, and I was not being supportive. I didn't enjoy puncturing her dream, but I felt she needed honesty from someone because she was incapable of being honest with herself. She felt she had to try, and she did. With agonizing results, I heard. Eventually the pain of reality convinced her to look for some other dream to follow. She may always regret never being able to realize her dream of becoming a ballerina. She should never regret her attempt to make it real.

I had a similar dream at her age. In my twenties, I imagined playing professional soccer for a career. I loved the game, and still do. I threw myself into a training program and managed to join a semiprofessional soccer team, where I played well enough to earn a tryout with a pro team. That's when reality hit me as hard as it hit my friend the hopeful ballerina. I was good, but not nearly good enough to compete among the pros. I was told I could probably qualify as a second-string player on a semipro team. That was a little flattering but not at all what I was aiming for. I felt that if I was going to play at something, I wanted to play to win, and I abandoned the idea.

Giving up on your dreams is hard, especially if you have yet to discover all your special skills and abilities. We humans are incredible creations, as unique as snowflakes, and each of us is great at something. Tragedy occurs when we never discover just what it is. Or never go seriously looking for it.

In a world that believes *You can be anything you want to be,* those decisions by the dancer and me may sound suspiciously like quitting. That's a sobering thought. You are not supposed to quit.

You are supposed to keep working until your dream becomes reality. That's a fine idea, until reality gives you a swift kick in the butt and you realize it's time to find some other dream to follow.

Yet I still hear people preach "Never give up!," suggesting that those who shift their goals elsewhere are quitters. Maybe so. Except that too-tall dancers are not meant to be ballerinas, and too-slow soccer players are not meant to play at the pro level. At some point we all need to acknowledge the narrow line that separates the fanatical from the foolish. When this happens, don't change your determination to succeed; change your direction toward success.

In current business circles, a change in course is known as a pivot. You are not giving up and you are certainly not abandoning your dream. You are recognizing that success doesn't lie in quite the same spot that it once did. It has moved, and the only way to reach it is to make a similar move, pivoting to go north by northwest instead of due north.

There is no shame in changing course when aiming for success. It can be both a source of pride and a demonstration of wisdom.

Accepting what you are capable of doing well, based on your physique and mental abilities, narrows your horizon. That's a good first step. Because the shorter list helps you focus on things that excite you. You can stop dreaming and start doing.

If your passion is playing music; performing theatrics; painting in oils; or, on a more down-to-earth level, assembling and balancing columns of figures (yes, there are passionate accountants), you know where to turn.

It's easy if the passion is strong and readily defined. Yours may be more difficult to identify. Perhaps you love meeting people, learning their needs, and finding ways to help meet them. Or teaching the difference between similar products and processes. Or exploring aspects of psychology in a business relationship. Or being involved on a person-to-person level in business, where you are encouraged to make on-the-spot decisions to reach your goal.

Or how about this: you thrive on challenges and competition. Maybe not the sports or athletic variety, but on the chance to pace yourself at something, always intent on improving your score no matter how it's measured. Next time you see a marathon race passing through your town or on television, ask yourself how many of the runners are seriously intent on finishing first. My guess is fewer than two dozen or so. The rest of them are more interested in setting a personal best time, hoping to cut a few minutes off their previous runs. That's a legitimate goal, and one that can fuel a runner's passion.

Most of us relate to these kinds of challenges. They define us as people who accept the reality that everything changes, including ourselves. Personal growth involves something more than physical measure, after all. The act of becoming better at anything— faster, smoother, higher, smarter—is a means of achieving success while avoiding the risk of a wasted life.

I need to pause here and admit that this chapter may involve a leap of faith for many people. Why? Because I've been discussing the inevitability of change, and change can be a frightening proposition—especially if it involves your career, or serious thoughts you may have about finding a new one.

We fear change because change involves the future, where the roots of all fears are found. Nothing in the past can hurt us, but the future may be painful. If you bear the scars of failure and frustration in your career or personal life, you may fear that more of the same lies somewhere in your future as well. That's understandable. But the difference between a painful past and an unknowable future is right in front of you. It is today, the here and the now. This can be your pivot point, the place where you take charge of your life to both put the past behind you and shape the future ahead of you, keeping it free of everything but satisfaction and achievement.

My stories in this book may motivate you to take the first step toward carving a new, more satisfying life. I hope this happens, although the most I can do on these pages is spark your ambition.

One of the most important qualities we can have when setting out to shape our career and our life is belief in ourselves. Believing in yourself is essential, but you need to recognize the difference between self-belief and self-delusion. One is vital. The other is dangerous.

We encountered self-delusion earlier. It occurs when your dreams overrun reality. A simple explanation of this is dreaming you will win millions by winning a lottery. Dream on, and buy a lottery ticket now and then if you like. But if in your dream you ignore the multimillion-to-one odds that your number will be drawn, prepare yourself for disappointment.

Avoid self-delusion by looking closely at where and who you are today. Consider your age, your education, your personal responsibilities, your health, and your economic status. Look at them realistically. You can still—and should—believe in yourself. But now you know where you are and how far you have to travel. It's like directories in a shopping mall that have an arrow pointing to a location and announcing *You are here.* You need that information. If you don't know where you are when you start, how can you tell where you are going?

You also must hold on to your self-belief because the road to success is not paved with encouragement. It's crowded with people who have set out on the same journey as you and became lost, discouraged, or frightened. They'll be eager to warn that you will become as disenchanted as they are. Instead of believing them, you will need to believe in yourself more than ever.

I met some of those people years ago, when I changed my career and my life along with it. Whenever I described my vision and how I would achieve it, I would be told I was naïve and foolish, and I should give it up in favor of something with less risk and more security. Among one of their observations would be my lack of cash and my few contacts in business. "You need money to make money," I would be reminded, along with "It's not what you know, it's who you know."

These clichés might have discouraged me if I didn't have such strong belief in myself and my abilities. If it would take money to get started, then I would make it somewhere else, in some other kind of work. And if becoming successful meant knowing people, I would become the guy other people wanted to know. Finally, I was often told it would take a long time to reach the level of success I was aiming for. If that was the case, I thought, I had better get started *now*.

If you're ready to get started, there's probably no better time than now. Here are some hints to guide you down the path, whatever kind of business you may choose.

Start by being honest with yourself. Know what it takes to make you happy, and admit your limitations as well as your goals and skills. Having a vision and seeking to fulfill it are wonderful, but fooling yourself about your chance of success is risky. It's fine to want a job at a large legal firm, for example, but unless you have a law degree from a fancy school, your chances are probably zero. So what do you do? You can pivot toward a job with a similar function and status, perhaps working as an intern in a government department or public service organization, where you can build a reputation as someone who can handle challenging assignments. Your career may not be material for a John Grisham novel, but you'll enjoy similar satisfaction.

You'll also have to accept fear and find courage. Courage is not the absence of fear; it is the power to do things in the *presence* of fear, and do them well. People often tell me that it must be wonderful to have achieved so much success that I needn't fear the same things that frighten others. Well, they're wrong. I worry about things as much as almost anyone else—things I need to handle and things I have no control over.

You will also need to ignore the "I wish I had . . ." syndrome that keeps reminding you of the chances you have lost and the time you have wasted. Making a career change often involves rejecting much of your working life to that point. Don't waste time regretting the fact that you didn't make the move earlier, and refuse to beat yourself up about it. Along the way you gained knowledge and experience. Now is the time to use them.

Changing careers brings a whole new raft of options that are worth exploring. This is worthwhile because making a major change is naturally uncomfortable at the beginning. You can raise your comfort level by being aware of all the new choices you have and selecting the most promising among them. Warning: don't make the mistake of dwelling too long on this process, which can lead to "paralysis by analysis," which happens when you focus too long on things that can go wrong. At some point you need to admit you cannot anticipate all the bad things that might occur, and start taking action anyway. There is never any certainty of success in business or in life except this one: if you don't make an effort to realize your ambition, you will join all the others through history who, at the end of their lives, were forced to admit "I never even tried."

Share your concerns with people who will listen carefully to you and take your misgivings seriously. It's not necessary to ask their advice (although you're almost certain to receive it). If you are close to someone who once made a change similar to yours, talk to them about the way they handled their concerns. Talking about our fears is the best way of banishing them. Locked up in our minds, they are deadly; out in the sunshine of honest reality, they weaken and die.

You also need to prepare yourself to accept the messy parts of switching careers. Stuff happens. Sometimes it's messy stuff that you didn't expect and don't need. When this occurs, just clean up the mess and keep going. Good stuff can happen as well. That's what you should be prepared for—the unexpected windfall or golden opportunity that can accelerate your career and speed your way to success.

Plan on being a lifelong learner. Because you need to be. And you will need to know how to bounce back from time to time. Among all the things that will happen when starting out as an entrepreneur or a professional salesperson, here's one you can count on: you will make mistakes. No one avoids them entirely in business, in sports, or in life generally. Mistakes injure your pride and sometimes your pocketbook. That's the bad news. The good news is: mistakes are an opportunity to learn from experience, understand why they happened, and ensure that they do not happen again.

So be prepared to pivot. The path to success is rarely straight and short. It includes turns, switchbacks, and detours. Take the turns when you must, get back on the straight when you can, and always keep your momentum moving forward.

Finally, one more time: be realistic about your chances of success. I dealt with my dream of playing professional soccer when I was in my twenties. I didn't make it come true, but at least I chose the best time to try. Ten years later my efforts would have been somewhere between laughable and tragic. Never let go of your dreams, but always hold on to your sanity.

A final thought: if the idea of leaving your current job to start a new career still sounds like "quitting" to you, remember that it does not have to be a total turnaround. You could swing to a different function in the same industry you're in now, assuming a different role perhaps with the same employer. Or maybe you want to make a total change of direction toward where you believe your interests and your future lie. Either way, this should not label you as a "quitter." Call it pivoting, call it refocusing, call it shifting direction. Whatever name you choose, if the personal and material rewards appeal to you, you are pursuing your passion.

And there is never, ever anything wrong with that.

Ten Things You Need to Do When Making a Change in Your Life

1. *Be disciplined*—develop and maintain a work ethic.
2. *Be focused*—concentrate on the task at hand; the greater the challenge, the sharper the focus.
3. *Be competitive*—welcome competition and accept that

life rarely offers something of value that someone else will not try to get for themselves.

4. *Be resourceful*—use every asset available to you.

5. *Be passionate*—the more you believe in your product and yourself, the more successful you'll become.

6. *Be critically minded*—assume the attitude that lets you "think outside the box" when needed.

7. *Be persistent*—prepare yourself to hear no, but never let it discourage you.

8. *Be curious*—look for new ways to learn about customers, their concerns, their business, and their personalities.

9. *Be confident*—without being arrogant.

10. *Be happy*—try to be the source of joy for others; more than almost any other personal quality, this will attract others to you.

ELEVEN

The 80/20 Rule and How
It Rules Life

Earlier, I mentioned that while working for the collections agency I discovered that 20 percent of the people who owed money would never pay their debt under any circumstances. It made sense, then, to focus my efforts on the 80 percent who would pay at least a portion.

Later I learned that the 80/20 split is almost as predictable and universal as the law of gravity. It even has a name: the Pareto Principle (also known as the Law of the Vital Few), named for Vilfredo Pareto, who discovered it. Pareto was an Italian engineer born in 1848, and a pretty brilliant guy. Besides having a Ph.D. in engineering and lecturing in economics at universities in Florence and Switzerland, he wrote several books on subjects as wide-ranging as sociology and political science. Yes, your classic academic overachiever.

Here's what made him famous:

In 1906, while researching property ownership in Italy, Pareto discovered that 20 percent of the population owned 80 percent of the country's land. Interesting, he thought, but at the time it didn't appear to signify much. A few days later while tending his vegetable garden, Vilfredo noticed that 20 percent of the pea pods produced 80 percent of the peas. Was this a co-incidence? It had to be. What could pea production possibly have to do with land ownership?

Still, the similarity intrigued him, and Pareto began digging into the economic side of things, one of his specialties. He was stunned by what he found. The 80/20 ratio kept popping up in economics, biology, politics, and almost everywhere he looked, well beyond property and pea pods.

The principle was easy to discover but difficult to believe. He needed proof, so he created a mathematical formula to confirm its existence and predict its outcome. The formula is too complex for me or most other people to explain, but the effect of the Pareto Principle can be described this way:

> **Eighty percent of the effects of any activity comes from 20 percent of the cause.**

To put it in practical business terms:

> **Eighty percent of a company's business is made from 20 percent of its customers.**

Which leads to:

> **Eighty percent of a company's income is earned from 20 percent of its sales.**

The ratio is never this exact all the time, but it is consistent enough to be accepted as reality.

The Pareto Principle appears in surprising places. Speaking for my business, for example, of the millions of companies operating around the world only about 22 percent have annual sales above $1 billion, but they represent close to 80 percent of all computer spending.[1]

Company executives familiar with Pareto understand its significance. They can see its impact on their sales records:

> Eighty percent of their sales comes from 20 percent of their products.
>
> Eighty percent of their profits is earned during 20 percent of the time spent by their employees.

And so on. With these facts in hand, companies can find ways to maximize productivity and profits. Microsoft, for example, discovered that by fixing 20 percent of the bugs in its programs, it eliminated 80 percent of system errors and crashes. Guess where its programmers spent their time fine-tuning Microsoft products? And in 1992 the United Nations, in conjunction with Oxford University, reported that 20 percent of the population controlled 80 percent of the world's income.

The same principle applies to selling: 80 percent of a company's sales is made by 20 percent of its sales staff, which follows that 80 percent of sales commissions is paid to 20 percent of the salespeople. This tells you where both the money and the future are—the money from commissions, and the future from advancement and opportunity for the top 20 percent of salespeople. The remaining sales staff can be found among the 80 percent scrambling for the leftover 20 percent of sales. Why? Because they

---

1. Some industries knew about the 80/20 ratio long before the people involved realized it could be explained with a mathematical formula. The first thing that marketers and advertisers in the beer industry are told, for example, is that 80 percent of the beer is consumed by 20 percent of the people.

are less efficient. Or they prefer to coast rather than pedal. Or maybe they never heard of Pareto.

Anyone sincere about making a successful career in business generally, and sales in particular, will never be satisfied occupying the loser column. In my opinion they should either aim to be among the 20 percent making 80 percent of the money . . . or look for some other career.

Is that too harsh? I don't think so. As I said earlier, anyone who sets out to launch a new business needs to know what the odds of achieving success are, and they are not very good. To serious entrepreneurs, this doesn't matter. If a chance of success exists and if they believe they have the skill, energy, and ambition to win, they will not be intimidated by the odds. There is no reward without risk.

I knew this when I launched my company and beat the odds. Was luck involved? Luck is always involved in new ventures. But something else was in play as well.

In addition to becoming wealthy, one of my dreams as a young man was to become a successful Hollywood actor. Yes, both dreams were obviously linked. I found myself an agent, went to several auditions, and managed to grab a few small roles in TV commercials. Most actors begin this way, and I might have been on my way to a very different career than the business I'm in now, but I'll never know because I gave up that particular ambition. As surprising as it may be to those who know me today, I just didn't like being in the limelight.

The production side of the film business appealed to me more than working in front of the camera, and I began moving in that direction. Thanks to a lucky break I became a TV field producer covering the 1984 Winter Olympics in Sarajevo. I was only twenty-two at the time, which made me one of the youngest Olympics producers in history. I enjoyed the job, earned praise for my work, and began dreaming of moving to Hollywood, where I would switch from producing to directing, and become the next Martin Scorsese. Soon, I believed, I would be heading for California to cruise through Beverly Hills wearing sunglasses and a million-dollar smile—I could *feel* it. Without doubt, my dream of working in the movie business was going to come true. Except it didn't.

Using my experience at the Olympics as leverage, I worked my way up from small film production jobs until I was hired to work on a major movie that I expected would catapult me to Hollywood.

The movie was to be directed by an actor named Tom Laughlin, who had written and starred in an earlier film about a Native American. The hero's name, Billy Jack, was also the movie's title. In the script, Billy Jack returns to his hometown from Vietnam as a hero. He has had it with war and wants only peace and justice. He is soon recruited to help protect herds of wild horses from being slaughtered for dog food. Seeing himself as a new kind of hero, he next defends a commune of peace-loving artists against violent right-wing extremists.

It was a classic good guys versus bad guys story with a lot of kung fu fighting, which was a novelty at the time. Maybe too much of a novelty. When *Billy Jack* failed to make much of an impact at the box office, Laughlin blamed the Hollywood studios, bought back the rights, and decided to distribute it himself. Thanks to some imaginative marketing efforts that included karate demonstrations and appeals to anti-establishment young people, the movie became a hit in its second release. In fact, from a production budget of $800,000 it eventually grossed almost $100 million,[2] making it one of the most successful independent movies of all time.

Laughlin used his profits to produce sequels to *Billy Jack,* with varying success. By the mid-1980s he was up to the fifth movie in the series, to be titled *The Return of Billy Jack.*

I was hired as third or fourth assistant director on this one, essentially a glorified production job with a fancy title. But I would be working directly with Laughlin, who, I assumed, would teach me about the business, recognize my talents and abilities, and open big doors for me in Hollywood.

From the moment I took the job I was warned that Laughlin was "a trifle eccentric," and soon discovered this was an understatement. The man was totally unpredictable. Some days he loved me, and other days he hated me. I was fired one day and rehired the next, over and over. It was an insane way to make a movie, but I assumed it was not all that unusual in the film business (it isn't). I also learned that working in movies meant you could go for months without work, then overnight find yourself working literally around the clock. I had never avoided hard work, but this was driving me crazy. Still, I figured I had no options if I were to become the Hollywood success I wanted to be, so I put up with it until the day Laughlin fired me for the last time. This time he did it in front of the entire crew, insulting me in a loud, angry voice until I said, "That's it for the movie business," and walked off the set. I never returned.

I went straight from the movie set to the small apartment I shared with my buddy Steve. Before I could give him the details of what had happened to me, Steve began telling me about *his*

---

2. Source: IMDb.

awful day. He explained that he had gone for a job interview with a new computer company and blown his chance to be hired. He wouldn't say why. Just that he and the company founder were "not a good fit." It would be a good job, Steve suggested, for somebody who wanted to break into the computer business on the ground floor.

This was the mid-1980s, when IBM and Apple were introducing their first personal computers, or PCs. Not everyone understood how much impact computers would make on society back then, but it was clearly a promising industry. Maybe, I thought, instead of Hollywood, my future lay with computers. Especially when Steve said the job paid a $30,000 annual salary, a large potful of money at the time. "What's this guy's name," I asked Steve, "and how can I get an interview?"

To say I knew nothing about computers is an understatement. I did know, however, that it sounded like a better place than Hollywood to start my career. After Steve gave me a name and phone number, I talked my way into a job interview the next morning.

The man launching the computer company was the first entrepreneur I ever met. He told me he had just left a good job at IBM, the eight-hundred-pound gorilla in the computer business at the time, to launch his own company. He had given up a handsome salary, a comfy office, and a lot of job security. Now he had an empty office, a few pieces of used furniture, and a bit of money to get started. He lacked many other things, including employees. I would be the first staff member in the company if he hired me. Which seemed unlikely. After all, I had nothing to bring to his business.

He, however, had much to bring to my career and life. I began asking questions about his plans and his determination to succeed by starting a business from scratch. The more I heard, the better I felt about abandoning my plans to become a film director. I didn't know where the movie business was going, but I could tell that the future was about to be built on computers and I wanted to be there when it happened. If I couldn't create a *Taxi Driver* or an *Apocalypse Now,* maybe I could create a computer business with my name on it.

Sitting across from the man who had left IBM with a vision to build and run his own show, I grew passionate about the idea. Here was a genuine entrepreneur with ambition and plans to become a success in the fastest-growing industry in the world. As he described his company and plans I blurted out, *"You have to hire me!"*

My outburst seemed to amuse him. "You are not in the least qualified for the job," he said, and he was smiling tightly. "You don't have either sales or computer experience, and you need both of them for this job." He began to stand, signaling the interview was over and it was time for me to leave.

I remained seated. "I'll work for free," I said, and meant it. "You're starting a business and you need help. I'll do whatever you need and I'll do it free. You won't have to pay me a cent."

"I can't hire you for free," he said. "If I pay you nothing, I can't depend on you."

This became one of those now-or-never moments. He was correct in his thinking, I knew, but wrong in his assumption, and I wanted to prove it. I held out my hand to shake his, looked him squarely in the eye, and said with all the sincerity I could dredge from inside myself, "Oh, you can count on me."

My words and my action impressed him. He shrugged, smiled, nodded, and put out his hand to shake mine, which is when I pulled my hand back. "On one condition," I said. "If I meet all your expectations from the beginning, in six months you pay me what I would have been paid if I'd had that experience when you hired me." I put out my hand again, and, to the surprise of both of us, he agreed.

I left his office determined to become the hottest new guy in the computer business. There would be, of course, the slight problem of having no income for six months to cover basic essentials such as food and rent. I drove to the hottest restaurant I knew in the trendiest part of town, convinced them to hire me as a waiter, and began working a shift from six P.M. to midnight. For the next six months, I learned about computers during the day, doing whatever needed to be done around the office, soaking up knowledge like a sponge. I was out the door at five o'clock, serving food and drinks at six, and putting in hours until well past midnight. Then I stumbled home, got a few hours of sleep, and started all over again the next day.

How did I get by with so little sleep? I had long ago decided that I would rather be tired than poor. I had also read somewhere that whatever your body does for twenty-one days in a row becomes a habit. So for twenty-one days after getting both jobs I used three alarm clocks to make sure that no matter how tired I might be when I went to bed, I was up and awake the next morning and at my computer job on time. It worked. The habit has stayed with me since. It's not that I don't want more sleep. It's just that I don't have time for it.

Time is the great equalizer in life. Everyone is given the same amount of time every day. It is up to us to use those hours according to our needs and wants. When we use it well, we profit in various ways. When we waste it, it is gone forever; time is not a replenishable resource.

Six months later I was paid the salary I had agreed to defer, and gave up my evening gig at the restaurant and bar. I had some cash; I had some time for myself; and, most important, I had the deep suspicion that my future was somewhere in the computer industry.

And it was.

TWELVE

All the Things About Selling That I Learned from Dancing— and Vice Versa

The connection between the ability to sell and the ability to maneuver your way through the twists and turns of life was never drawn into sharper focus for me than in my experience on *Dancing with the Stars*. Sounds vague? Not when you go a little deeper into things.

If *Shark Tank* is an entertainment vehicle that happens to be about business, *Dancing with the Stars* is entertainment that happens to be about dancing. This is not to say that the dancing is not demanding, because it is—more physically demanding to me than anything I have ever attempted. But neither show would succeed unless it entertained viewers from the first minute it appears on their TV screen. At the core of both shows is a commitment to being competitive. Everyone who glides, steps, or stumbles onto the floor in *Dancing with the Stars* must honestly want and truly believe that he or she has a chance at the top prize. I certainly did. And so did Mark Cuban, who preceded me on the show by four years.

A few weeks before my first appearance on the show I met

Mark at a Super Bowl party. "I hear a rumor you're appearing on *Dancing with the Stars*," Mark said to me. "Physically, it was one of the hardest things I've ever done, so good luck."

"Actually," I said, unable to resist ribbing him, "my only goal is to go farther than you did." Then I added, "Which shouldn't be that hard."

Mark gave me his *You've got to be kidding me* look, and informed me that he and Kym Johnson had made it to round 5 of the show. After viewing a video of Mark and Kym's performance, my confidence weakened a little. It didn't help when the other Sharks began teasing me about my chances of avoiding being dropped in the first round. Eventually the teasing ended, and some Sharks came to the studio to watch me dance and offer support. Best of all to me, Kym and I actually rose higher in the standings than Mark had, which gave me a few bragging rights.

The intensity of the competition and the need to succeed where others might have failed or, in this case, not come as close to total success as I did, are at the heart of my approach to business. Yes, appearing on *DWTS* was fun and, yes, it was educational and, yes, the experience was rewarding to me in many ways. But the attitude I carried with me onto the dance floor was closely related to the one I have when going into a sales situation: I know my steps, I know what I can bring to the deal, and I'm ready to deliver value. I'm also ready to have fun, something I try to inject into every sales presentation I make.

The link between dancing and selling isn't really such a stretch once you recognize that basic sales techniques are involved whenever we either express our needs, or are in a position to satisfy the needs of others. Like many things, we're not aware of the mechanics involved until they are pointed out to us.

If you love to dance . . . or even if you just love to watch other people dance . . . perhaps you'll see the links I discovered between them from my *DWTS* experience. Here they are:

You have ninety seconds to strut your stuff.

Hours of practice for *Dancing with the Stars* came down to a minute and a half for each dance in front of judges watching for every misstep.

It's all you need to let everyone know if you belong on the dance floor. Ninety seconds is about the same amount of time salespeople receive to make a positive first impression on a customer.

Keep your mouth shut and your eyes and ears open.

Talking to your partner while dancing may be romantic, but in competitive dancing you don't talk; you pay attention to the music, sense your partner's moves, and try to remember the steps you rehearsed. That's a good parallel between competitive dancing and effective selling. It might be stretching the point for salespeople to picture customers as their dance partners, and the music as their needs and wants. But it works for me.

You need a story to tell and rehearsals to tell it smoothly.

On *DWTS*, each dance needs a story and a setting. For our jive routine, Kym suggested we start with the two of us seated at a drive-in movie in an open 1950s-era convertible. This took a lot of time to set up and rehearse, but it proved perfect for the dance and added to the performance. My biggest concern was to avoid tripping when leaving the car.

When my sales staff and I make a major sales presentation, we spend extensive time planning, rehearsing, and preparing. And we always worry about tripping.

Never show pain or uncertainty.

During one of the last rehearsals for our tango dance, I pulled muscles in my shoulders and my hip. The pain was agonizing. Not only could I not imagine performing the dance, I couldn't walk. On the day of the performance my body still ached, and I thought there was no way we could perform our dance until I found a doctor to inject me with a painkiller. It took four shots of cortisone to deaden the soreness.

Neither of us mentioned it to the show producers or the other dancers, because we knew we couldn't expect either special treatment or a whole bunch of sympathy. That's how the show works. It's also how life works.

Later I learned that other dancers suffered pain at some point in the competition, and their partners knew about it. No one in the studio audience or viewers at home could tell. Once the cameras began rolling we all kept smiling. No one was aware of our pain, our nervousness, or any discomfort we felt. We were *selling* our performances, so we had to make everything look easy. Most of all, we had to look confident. Any suggestion that we were uncomfortable or uncertain would weaken that impression. The same display of poise is essential to making a sales pitch and in so many other parts of our lives.

Practice is fine, but performance is everything.

Of all the contestants during the season of *Dancing with the Stars* that I participated in, none was more charming than Patti LaBelle, who taught me a new lesson about selling.

I was wearing myself out mentally and physically by rehearsing as many as ten hours every day. Then I discovered that Patti refused to spend more than two hours a day practicing. She would begin each session by telling her professional partner, Artem Chigvintsev, "Here's the step I'm going to do. You come up with stuff to do around me." When I asked how she was winning over the judges and audience that way, she replied, "Honey, all the practice and rehearsal don't matter if you can't get it goin' on the floor when the camera starts rolling."

Patti, of course, was an experienced big-name performer who had been nominated for Emmy and Grammy Awards, starred in Broadway musicals, appeared in Hollywood movies, and authored her own biography. She even had a star on the Hollywood Walk of Fame. This woman knew about show business, and knew how to sell herself as a performer.

Her personality shone through the little mistakes she made. The night she performed the quick-step, she planned to kick off both shoes halfway through the dance. When only one shoe slipped off her foot, she finished her dance anyway, endearing herself to the audience and judges.

When the curtain comes up on some show-biz-style part of your life and cameras start rolling, nothing less than your best performance will do.

Of course, charm helps. It helps a lot.

Confidence can sell anything—even a bad salsa step.

During a break on our rehearsal once, I asked Kym to tell me the best way to judge the dancing ability of someone who was not a professional. Kym said, "You watch their eyes." Not their feet. Their eyes. People unsure of their dancing ability let their eyes wander because they're asking themselves, *Omigod, what do I do next??!!*

When you are secure in anything you do, your body—especially your eyes—conveys the feeling. Good salespeople sell their confidence along with whatever the customer is considering buying. Confidence, remember, inspires trust. And of all the qualities that salespeople need to build with their customers, none is more important than trust.

Building confidence in ourselves begins by convincing first ourselves and then the rest of the world that we *are* confident.

The better you get, the faster things move.

It sounds obvious to say that the more you perform something, the better you become at it. The better you are at anything in life, the shorter the amount of time it takes to do it. Things happen faster and with more accuracy when you improve your ability through sharper focus and frequent practice. Which, taken together, builds self-assurance.

There is always a new step to learn.

Kym and I didn't have time to dwell on any missteps we had made in a show. We put the memory out of our minds, because we had a new and entirely different step to practice and perform the following week.

It's a lesson worth remembering. We all experience failures in our lives; we just can't afford to dwell on them. All we can do is identify where and how we failed, choose the best way to avoid repeating it, then move on.

There will always be another chance to dance.

Know how the score is being kept.

All of us are judged by the things we do in life. The judges are our partners, our family, our friends, our business associates, our customers and clients, and our competitors. They assess us, just as we assess them. We never escape this kind of assessment, regardless of the biblical maxim about not judging lest we be judged ourselves. And we never know if we are being judged fairly unless we know how the score is being kept.

Dancing with the Stars is both a competition and popular TV entertainment. The dancers expect to be rated according to their skill on the floor, but the success of *DWTS,* like all mass entertainment productions, is judged by the size of the audience it attracts. And all audiences love a good story line.

Kym and I provided a great story line for the show over the first half-dozen episodes. To anyone who watched, it was apparent that we were falling in love, and the show producers made the most of it because it proved popular with the viewing audience. This undoubtedly influenced the number of votes we received, especially in the early stages. Viewers liked the idea of watching our relationship grow as much as they enjoyed watching our dance routines. We were realistic about the situation. I wasn't the most talented dancer in the competition, but I was having an incredible time! As much as we wanted to win, and as hard as we worked to earn high scores, we took it all in stride, realizing we were winning something greater than a mirror ball trophy.

As they say, that's show business. But there's a lesson here: whenever you are in a situation where you know your performance will be scored, learn how the score is being kept. And how much it can be influenced by things other than your performance.

Never forget your motivation.

There are periods in our lives when we doubt ourselves, especially when we do something important for the first time.

The first dance Kym and I performed was a cha-cha, and we decided to kick it off with a mock-up of *Shark Tank.* The story would begin with me sitting on a stage with four other Sharks, listening to Kym make her business pitch. Suddenly, captured by her beauty and charm, I would toss my pad and pencil aside, skip down from the stage to the floor, grab her hand, and the dance was on.

Through all the rehearsals I kept picturing myself stumbling down the stairs before I had a chance to dance a single step. There would be no retakes, I was informed. If I tripped over my feet, it would be broadcast worldwide, with multiple camera angles and slow-motion effects. Despite all my positive thinking, I couldn't wipe the image from my mind. Yet I had to, or I would never be able to perform the dance with confidence.

Sensing my nervousness during the commercial break just before our dance began, Kym pulled me aside and whispered to me, "I know you're nervous, but just remember why you are here."

I knew what she meant.

Soon after meeting each other, I had told Kym how much my mother enjoyed *Dancing with the Stars*. It had been her favorite program on television. Mother had never experienced anything remotely like the show when she was a young woman growing up in a rural Croatian village. The show was magical to her.

I imagined how proud Mother would have been to see me participating on it. All that I had achieved in business, on *Shark Tank,* and as an author would not have impressed her more than seeing me as a participant on *Dancing with the Stars.* It was the main reason I agreed to appear on the show.

So I was there because of my mother, and all that she meant to me. That's what Kym urged me to remember. When my cue arrived I kicked things off with confidence, almost leaping down the stairs to join Kym on the dance floor. I wore a smile on my face through every step, reminding myself why I was there, and how it would have thrilled my mother.

In the middle of so many things we do in our lives, it's easy to overlook the reasons we perform them in the first place. We need to remind ourselves of our motivation from time to time. Sometimes we can do this on our own. Sometimes we need another person who understands and cares enough to do it for us.

Make yourself comfortable.

Clothes don't make the man or woman, but they can make him or her feel at ease under pressure. If I make a sales presentation to a Silicon Valley company that designs video games, I might wear jeans and sneakers. Or not. Some young Internet-connected people expect those outside their industry to appear more establishment-oriented, because it suggests corporate stability and experience. If I showed up at a meeting dressed as though I'm hanging around the house on weekends, they could suspect that I'm not taking the meeting seriously. So here's my rule: when dealing with a defined segment of society, it pays to determine their wardrobe preference. Being dressed too casually or too formally for the setting will not make me comfortable. Worse, it may make the potential buyers uncomfortable.

The dance floor dictated a different approach. I wish I could have selected comfort over style when appearing on *Dancing with the Stars.* Three-inch heels and tight trousers looked good when doing the tango, and afterward I looked forward to sweatpants and sneakers. But I was dressed appropriately, which helped my comfort level.

Know when to follow and when to lead.

Most dance steps require the male to lead. Or appear to. In selling, the sales representative needs to respond to the customers' steps, following them (even while asking open-ended questions) until they sense that it's their turn to close the sale.

Remain in the moment.

Salespeople and competitive dancers need to push everything out of their minds—that argument with their partner, the pain in their shoulder, next week's dentist appointment—and pay attention to what is happening directly in front of them. Losing your focus on the dance floor in the middle of a complicated routine can lead to utter disaster. So can losing your thought in the middle of a sales pitch or in response to a customer's question.

Stay grounded.

Dance professionals tell me that many beginning dancers try to do too much too soon. Instead of keeping both feet on the floor during a samba or a rhumba, they attempt a spinning motion or some other move that makes them look silly instead of skilled. The same thing can happen when salespeople try going beyond their experience and confidence levels, trying to impress a customer with jargon or concepts they don't fully understand.

Know when to ask for help.

I watched professional dancers on *DWTS* assist each other in a warm and selfless manner. Salespeople should feel the same way. Not about competitors, but about people in their own firm who have advice to offer. Novices who are not competing directly against other salespeople should feel free to ask experienced colleagues for guidance when it's needed, reminding themselves that we learn nothing when we ask nothing.

Smile and have fun.

With the exception of serious classical ballet routines, all great dancers appear to enjoy themselves as they move across the floor together. Carrying that same approach to a work environment is a great idea. "Maybe they're having fun," I hear you say. "But they're dancing and I'm talking about *work*. I'm talking about my *job*! How can that always be fun?"

If the concept of having fun on the job doesn't sound sensible, it's time to reassess your logic. And maybe your job. Yes, it can produce stress and insecurity. But displaying dissatisfaction or impatience with and general dislike for your work is one of the best ways I know to ensure failure. Which can lead to getting fired. I won't presume to say you can find fun in everything you do every day you're on the job. If your job is so tedious and soul-destroying, however, that you never find a reason to smile, laugh, and feel a sense of pride in your work, you are in the wrong job. Or working for the wrong company. Or have the wrong approach to life generally.

Everyone does things they enjoy better than things they dislike. That's not just my view as an individual, it's also my view as an employer. I want people on my staff who find it easy to smile on the job, and who believe their work is the source of much of their happiness.

If that's you, fine.

If it's not you, look for other work. Now.

THIRTEEN

Five Things Every Salesperson Needs to Know

Earlier I stated that there is no such thing as a natural salesperson. No one is "born" to start making a sale, but almost everyone can learn and apply the basic rules of successful selling. Moving from a novice to a sales professional takes acquiring some basic knowledge, and none is more critical than this:

> **To buyers, the sales experience—the relationship and exchange between the buyer and the seller—is as important and influential as the product's price and performance.**

Our lives, and the joy we get from them, are dependent on the number and quality of the relationships we experience. Nothing I can think of will color your life, for good or bad, more than the relationships you build and the ones that either escape you or that you destroy. And we never outgrow this need.

I have achieved much in my businesses, and I take great pride in it. But my happiness depends more on the people whose love and trust I value than on the amount of financial success I have reached. In moments of total truth, I expect that everyone in business would agree totally with that statement. Business has as much to teach us about life, I believe, as life has to teach us about business. And neither can exist and be truly rewarding without the relationships we build.

Selling involves establishing a relationship that leads to the transfer of buyers' money in exchange for a valued service or benefit. This applies equally to a $100 million aircraft purchase and a $50 toaster sale. The relationships may differ in number, size, and style, but at their heart they're pretty much the same.

The comparison reminds me of driving a car. If I drive to the grocery store, there are many contrasts between that shopping trip and the two-hundred-mile-per-hour auto races I once competed in. But in both cases I had to steer the car, brake when needed, watch for other drivers, and know exactly where I wanted to go. Other things were different, including my speed and the risk I was taking, but I was still driving a car. A whole team of engineers, aviation experts, purchasing agents, and lawyers may be involved in the aircraft sale, and one minimum-wage clerk with the toaster. The aircraft sale could take weeks, months, or even years to complete, and the toaster just a few seconds. But some relationship or connection is always made before money changes hands.[1]

Good salespeople find a way to establish and maintain a relationship according to the situation and the products being sold. They begin with the things they need to *know,* and here are five of them:

---

1. What about Amazon and similar Internet marketers? They establish relationships in different but effective ways, including professionally crafted advertisements on their site and, thanks to cookies, frequent reminders of products they suspect you can't live without, based on your established buying patterns and history. That's a relationship of sorts.

1.   They understand what they are selling. And why.

Of course they need to know more than their customer about the product or service being sold. But the best don't stop there. They also know their competition in as much detail as they can gather, and all the factors that make the competition more or less appealing than their own product. Few things these days are obviously superior in every measure. By knowing the competitor's advantages, they are prepared to counter them with their own exclusive benefits.

A competitor's price advantage might be balanced with a feature that is equally attractive, such as a longer warranty period or some other benefit not linked to price.

Just as essential as knowing the features of the product is understanding the reason for owning it in the first place. I have been surprised by salespeople who know—or claim to know—every sales feature of their product yet have never seen or used it.

New car salespeople looking for buyers of off-road vehicles should not only drive a demonstrator on the highway; they should get behind the wheel and experience handling the car in a wide range of road conditions. They may be able to quote specifications and features all day long, but if the potential buyer asks how it handles when crossing a dry creek bed, describing a trip on the interstate won't prove helpful. In fact, it may prove counterproductive. Saying, "Oh, it's just fine in a dry creek bed" is not very convincing. Saying, "I crossed a dry creek bed up near Sunset Mesa, down four feet on one side and about six feet on the other, and it just walked over them like it was tarmac," not only conveys an advantage, it also can launch a selling relationship.

The same tactic applies to items being sold that make personal experience difficult to acquire or explain, but the parallel remains. If the product is a complex business program for accountants, good salespeople learn to understand how the major commands work, what the results look like on the screen, and how the program compares with the competition.

I know some salespeople who still believe they can make a sale just by quoting the specifications, using a promotional brochure as a guide. The "20 percent" salespeople—the ones who score 80 percent of the sales—go much farther.

Retail salespeople cannot know all the features and benefits of all the products in their inventory. But understanding and explaining just one feature—even if it's the manufacturer's reputation for quality—can help close a sale.

2. **They know the differences among features, advantages, and benefits—and the power of emotion.**

Features are qualities of a product that distinguish it from the competition. In many cases, the primary feature is the reason the product was developed in the first place. Apple's iPod, for example, stores thousands of songs in a small package for near-instantaneous access. That was the basis of its creation, and continues to be its key feature.

Advantages describe the connection between the product features and the benefits they provide the owner. The big feature of the iPod, remember, is its ability to store an entire music collection in a pocket-size device; its advantage is that the owner has his or her entire musical library always at hand.

Benefits are whatever the buyer understands he or she will enjoy from owning the product. They measure the product's appeal and value. Compare the iPod's features and advantages. The benefit it offers is the ability for owners to listen to their music anytime and anywhere—which, in the final analysis, is all that owners really care about.

While a salesperson rhymes off a product's advantages, the customer listens for its benefits. Once music lovers of a certain age grasped the iPod's features, they made the leap to the benefits all on their own. Products that are less revolutionary demand a more complicated sales pitch. Going back to car sales: anyone selling hybrid cars would comment on its most obvious feature, explaining how it uses both gasoline and electricity for power. The advantage of this, of course, is better gas mileage; the benefit is lower fuel costs.

The path from feature to advantage to benefit is not always so smooth; sometimes it can be challenging to follow. While I'm still on cars, imagine trying to sell a vehicle whose key feature is the engine, which develops five hundred horsepower and can go from standing still to sixty miles an hour in less than five seconds. An impressive feature, right? But what's the benefit, and to whom does it appeal? Many people would not see such massive power as a benefit; they might consider the car dangerous to drive.

When the benefits of a product or service are not immediately obvious, salespeople need to tip the buying decision in their favor by confirming that the customer understands and appreciates the benefit.

If the product is a cell phone with a feature that includes linkage to the newest design generation, the salesperson can point out how this offers faster access to Web applications than other, less expensive models. Some technology freaks may be sufficiently impressed by this feature alone to make a purchase. Others will respond to the faster speed with "So what?" That's when the feature and the benefit need to be explained in basic terms, pointing out, for example, that the faster phone will more quickly connect with the GPS function if the owner gets lost.

That may sound like a relatively minor benefit, but it carries something all benefits need: an emotional quotient. Here is a hard-and-fast rule: *When it comes to completing a sale, emotion trumps logic every time.* The fast Internet feature of the newer telephone sounds appealing, but the benefit of using the GPS to find your location quickly if you are lost taps into something deep and motivating.

Matching benefits to buyer is almost always a winner. Mismatching them can be a disaster. Cybergeeks will drool over the chance to have a smartphone that operates at twice the speed of their friends' smartphones. Middle-aged and older folk are likely to recoil from the idea of owning a car with a five-hundred-horsepower engine.

When the customer understands the product's features, appreciates its advantages, and responds to the benefits, the tipping point will be the emotional response to these qualities. Good salespeople know how the emotion factor triggers sales and know the words to convey it when needed.

Here are a few key emotionally connected words and the response they can generate among buyers:

Comfort—customers will experience luxury and contentment.

Convenience—they will have an important item close at hand and easily accessible.

Efficiency—they will be productive with their time and energy.

Fashion—they will be in style and up to date with their friends.

Fun and happiness—they will experience the sum of all the positive emotional benefits associated with the product.

Leisure—they will have more time to relax and enjoy life.

Peace of mind—they will not worry about some aspect of life that threatens to trouble them.

Security—they and their family will be safe from dangers such as weather, crime, financial stress, and so on.

Status—their friends will look up to and even envy them.

Success—they will have achieved (or appear to have achieved) some important goal in life.

3. They learn everything possible about buyers and their interests.

This may sound a little over the top to someone selling in retail. A customer who walks into the store looking for a dining room set or new laser printer may not provide much opportunity for learning about her and her interests, so why even try? And how?

The "why" is easy; effective selling depends on building a relationship with the customer, however brief it may be. The "how" can be a little more challenging, but there are ways to get it done.

When I was in university I worked for a few months as a salesman in a high-end menswear store. We carried high-fashion lines such as Hugo Boss, Armani, and Canali, which were great value but beyond the price range of many shoppers. We were never advised to dismiss anyone entering the store who, at first glance, appeared not to fit the buyer profile for these lines. But it helped if we could quickly get past any uncertainty about them as serious potential customers. It was a variation on the Pareto Principle; if 80 percent of the sales were made to 20 percent of the customers, it was a certainty that those 20 percent had above-average incomes and taste in clothing. All we had to do was identify them early and focus our sales efforts on them.

Where male customers were concerned, we made a point of checking their wristwatch and their shoes. If we saw a Rolex or a watch of similar value on their wrists, we would assume they were in the sought-after 20 percent category. A pair of expensive leather shoes, and not some beat-up Nikes, lifted their value a little higher. Lacking either of these would not disqualify them, but they represented the first step in getting to know the customers and understanding their needs and interests.

Retail sales are challenging when acquiring knowledge of buyers and building some kind of relationship with them. Corporate sales are both more complex and accessible than retail when it comes to relationship building. More time is usually available in corporate sales because the purchases are almost always larger and more involved than in retail. In a retail operation, only a few seconds may be available for the salesperson to make both a connection and a positive impression. In the corporate world, several visits may enable the salesperson to create and nurture a relationship that could lead to a sale. A lot of information on the corporate customer is available from annual reports, news clippings, and other sources, but much is confidential and difficult for an outsider to access.

When I make a major sales presentation on behalf of my company, our success or failure at securing a contract can be measured in millions of dollars. The time and effort we invest in our presentation for a business that size is extensive and often exhausting. But the potential reward is impressive. Top salespeople know just how much time and effort can be justified, and they don't invest just enough to make it all worthwhile; they go well beyond that point.

Like so many aspects of selling, the best professionals know and apply certain methods to make their pitches more effective. Sometimes they employ devices to motivate themselves.

One salesman I know starts to tailor his sales pitch by assuming he is working not to make a sale to the company but to obtain a senior position within it. If he were applying for an executive position with the firm, he reminds himself, he would want to know more about the company than just the products it markets. He would be interested in the competition, the recent successes and failures, the backgrounds of the top executives, the locations of the branch offices, the stock market performance if it's a publicly traded company, and more. Much of this kind of data is available in company brochures, annual reports, and business media articles, as well as on the Internet. He gathers everything he can find, as though he were selling himself to the company as a potential employee rather than selling the company a product or service. Instead of hiring my salesman friend, the client signs a purchase order to buy the product he's selling. The let's-get-a-job game the salesman is playing doesn't just guide him toward important information he can use; it also provides a new angle to what he learns of the company, perhaps offering a view of its needs that he would not have seen from a strict let's-make-a-deal approach.

It's difficult to believe a salesperson would not take the time to learn about the customer before making a presentation, but it still seems to happen. I'm often surprised at how little information some salespeople are satisfied with knowing. Assuming that the size of the potential sale justifies the effort, every relevant fact available should be gathered and assessed. When it comes to preparing a business-to-business sales presentation, there is no such thing as useless information.

A fine idea, perhaps, but time and resources are limited. Salespeople may have as little as a day or two to do their research, decide on a strategy, and create their pitch. The best of them know the key facts to nail down and make use of when planning their presentation. They include:

- *Their firm's history with the client.* Have we sold to them before? What product category was it in? What kind of feedback—satisfaction or problems—did the client provide?
- *The client's product lines and categories.* What's new? What markets do they serve? What is their market share? How will our product fit in the mix? What are the outstanding features and benefits of the products? How are they priced compared with the competition?
- *Sales trends affecting the client's success.* Where are they headed?
- *The client's marketing goals and strategies.* How do they promote their products? To whom? In what area will our product assist them?
- *Distribution networks.* How are the products distributed? Who and where are the key dealers, brokers, wholesalers, etc.?
- *Top executives.* What are their names, backgrounds, and primary duties? How familiar are they with our firm's products, services, and key personnel?

4. They discover what clients may know about *them*.

When it comes to vendor knowledge, business buyers today are more informed and better connected than they were even just a few years ago. They are also more impatient, more overloaded, and more risk-averse. Just to complicate things, buying decisions are spread among more people, which means more people have access to the same pool of data. And they make their decision later in the sales process. Not long ago, the first step made by prospective buyers in need of a product or service was to say, "Let's call the people who sell this product/service and see what they can tell us about it." Today it's more like, "Now that we've narrowed the choice down to a couple of suppliers who look good, let's bring them in and get down to serious business."

No matter who calls whom initially—the salesperson makes a cold call to a prospect, or the prospect calls in response to a firm's promotion efforts—customers will likely learn as much about the vendor's company as the vendor will uncover about theirs. Maybe more. They'll be checking out the vendor's products, services, pricing, history, and reputation. Especially reputation.

Salespeople need to begin by acknowledging that the buyer is at least somewhat familiar with their product's features and benefits and with the company behind it. They'll probably know the vendor's relative strengths and weaknesses compared with its competitors and will be at least as interested in the weakness of the vendor's pitch as its strength. If this includes product failures or other missteps made in the past, the vendor sales staff needs to be prepared to deal with them quickly, getting them off the table and out of the picture early. Bad news must never be ignored or denied; it must be dealt with and lead to building a case based on the product's positive qualities.

5.   They review their sales pitch and visualize their success.
After all the years on *Shark Tank* with Kevin, Daymond, Mark, Barbara, and others, I continue to be surprised, shocked, and disappointed—sometimes to the point of outrage—at the

poor quality of many presentations made to us. Why the outrage? Because these people are looking for hundreds of thousands— even millions—of our dollars, and they often behave as though they are asking for spare change.

We are businesspeople searching for a business opportunity. We can tolerate a sales pitch that is less than exceptional if the story promises to make us money. But many of the pitches are made by people stumbling and fumbling over the facts, or lacking answers to key questions such as, What are your annual sales to this point?, How much margin do you make on your sales?, and What do you plan to do with the money if we give it to you?

The questions may make the pitchers flustered, irate, defensive, or sometimes all three, and we Sharks may appear to be bullying them. But we're not. I hate bullies. I know what it's like to have someone harass you, and being a bully is never my intent (I can't speak for Kevin O'Leary, of course . . .). Each session of *Shark Tank* requires as many as twelve hours in the studio. After six or eight hours, we Sharks become cranky, hungry, and impatient. When someone who appears to have created his or her pitch over a cup of coffee that morning shows up in front of us, we become annoyed.

We are always impressed (and often surprised) with someone who has anticipated our concerns and questions and is prepared to answer them directly. No fudging, no promises, no excuses—just a direct response to the kinds of things we need to know before we pull out our checkbooks. Can a great pitch turn a mediocre idea into something we would like to seriously consider as an investment? You bet it can. Knowledge and enthusiasm among entrepreneurs making a pitch have a value that cannot be ignored.

When developing a presentation there is no need to assume

the buyer is tired, cranky, hungry, or impatient like we Sharks are at the end of a long day (although it's not a bad idea to be prepared). It's essential, however, to anticipate tough questions and to be ready to answer them directly.

I'm not the guy to explain all the psychology behind it, but research has revealed that people facing a major test of their abilities have a better chance of success if they allow themselves to visualize the event beforehand. It appears to work as well for professional athletes and stage performers as it does for salespeople. I often take time before a sales meeting to sit quietly alone and imagine making my sales presentation, anticipating questions and responding to them and ultimately shaking hands on a closed deal. My actual presentation may not flow just as I pictured it. But you would be surprised how well it prepares me for the real thing . . . and how often I am able to make the sale.

FOURTEEN

Five Things That Everyone in Sales Needs to Do

You are onstage. The overture ends. The curtain rises. The spotlight is on you. Everyone in the room has come to see and hear you, because you have the leading role. That's what it can feel like when making a sales pitch to a group of people responsible for a corporate buying decision. You know (or should know) the lines to deliver and the character you're playing. Stage fright? Forget it. You're a performer.

They are waiting. You smile. You nod. And you begin to speak.

This isn't Broadway or live television. This is business, and no one ever scored a victory in every business decision they made. Still, good salespeople understand that their job involves some kind of performance. The best of them play it up and become stars by adapting their inner ham to the situation. Most of this involves five actions taken before and during a sales presentation. Once again, the number of steps involved depends on what they are selling and to whom they are selling it. The basic rules, however, still apply.

1. They leave their ego in their briefcase.

At first glance, this may not sound sensible. Isn't a strong ego an important part of everyone's drive to succeed, and every actor's need to perform? And shouldn't every salesperson be focused on success?

Yes, yes, and yes. But a big ego is like a large truck— sometimes you don't need to roar down the road with a ton of cargo on board. Sometimes you just need to drive quietly, save fuel, and not disturb people. Or set aside the truck and ride a bicycle. Or get out and walk.

Salespeople who rely on their ego to carry them through a presentation risk letting it take over the meeting.

Ego is the driving force in everyone's career, not to mention his or her life in general. Ego defines who and what a person is and underlies a person's sense of self-worth. We all need ego to propel us through life with pride and identity, as long as we can keep it under control. Without question, we use it when making a sales pitch, quietly pushing us toward completing the sale. We just don't need it sitting in a chair next to us.

Problems with our ego arise when we sense either a threat from the other side or a weakness on our part. When that happens, it's the ego's job to do whatever is necessary to boost our confidence. But we are not in front of sales prospects to boost our self-esteem. Just the opposite, in fact. The goal should include boosting *prospects'* self-esteem by showing how they will benefit by choosing to buy. It also helps if they believe their self-worth will rise with their decision to buy whatever we are selling— not to mention their esteem in the eyes of their colleagues and bosses, if it's a corporate purchase.

When a comment made by a salesperson during a presentation is questioned by the customer, or when the salesperson's senses suggest that the pitch is not making the right impression, the ego wants to assert itself. This can encourage the salesperson to exaggerate the product's performance or value. It can lead to half-truths, outright lies, and manipulation in an attempt to improve the salesperson's chance of closing a sale. Raising the salesperson's self-worth will become the primary goal. That's the ego's job, after all. But it's not the salesperson's.

Things can go astray easily.

An oversize ego does not accept the prospect of failure. Experienced salespeople expect this can happen with any sales pitch they make. They don't need it, they don't like it, and they will do everything to avoid it. But letting one's ego assume control can lead to more than failure. It can lead to disaster.

Oversize egos can achieve many things. They can even make a TV personality popular. Many viewers of *Shark Tank* talk to me about Kevin O'Leary, saying, "He has such a big ego! Doesn't he get on your nerves?"

I tell them, "No, because we all have big egos. You need one to feel confident in front of the television camera, knowing millions are listening to your every word and watching your every move. Kevin's is just . . . different."

It takes a healthy ego to become a television personality and a successful salesperson. Not necessarily a giant ego. Just a healthy one that says *I can do this and do it well.* The most valuable benefit of a healthy ego is that it bolsters confidence and displays it to the sales prospect. This is critical—if salespeople don't appear confident in themselves, their product, and their sales message, customers will have little or no confidence in *them,* and that's certain death to closing the sale. What they *don't* need—what they must avoid at all costs—is any hint of arrogance.

How do good salespeople control their ego? They start by being open-minded about themselves and honest about their customer's needs and wants. They heighten their curiosity about the people on the other side of the table. They stroke a prospect's ego while holding theirs in check.

We value our relationships with people in sales just as much as we value them in other parts of our lives. But it's *people* we need to deal with. Nobody's interested in dealing with egos.

2.   They work at building relationships.

It's easy to be cynical about the relationships that salespeople build with customers, especially at the corporate level, where the sales can be measured in millions of dollars. At its root, relationship building can resemble manipulation. Actually, it's not. Building a relationship with sales prospects recognizes that companies don't buy from other companies; *people buy from people.* The second part of this truth is: *they buy from people they know and trust.*

We're not searching for a new BFF when we start building a relationship with a customer. We're building trust and knowledge between us that the customer will rely on to make an intelligent decision. Trust in a sales relationship results from things such as shared values and common understanding, not sales pressure.

There are no hard-and-fast rules for building a relationship in this context, because each of us is unique. There are ways, however, to begin paving the way toward a relationship with a new prospect. They should be used sparingly and according to the prospect's values, interests, and character, ensuring that the relationship flows easily between both parties and does not leap to new, higher levels like stages in a video game.

How do top salespeople build relationships with key clients? They begin by recognizing that everyone is a unique individual, which means they avoid pigeonholing and a formula approach.

They may, however, employ some familiar means, or a combination of them, including:

- *Looking for mutual interests.* If the salesperson is a golfer and sees a golf photo or award on the wall (or sometimes a bag of clubs in a corner), they're on their way. They don't need to describe every course they have played or every hole they birdied. They just make the connection, wait for a response, listen closely, and let it flow from there.
- *Offering a gift.* This one must be used with caution. Nobody can buy a relationship in life or in business with a gift, and going overboard by flooding a prospect with gifts can be disastrous. So when should it happen? It depends on the relationship and the gift. Sometimes recognizing a personal goal that the client has achieved, in or out of business, is a gift in itself.
- *Asking their opinion on some neutral topic.* Valuing a customer's insights while perhaps exploring other things the two of you may have in common is a good way to develop a relationship. Politics and religion, of course, should be avoided at all costs.
- *Conveying compliments carefully.* Trust isn't built with dishonesty, but a sincere compliment is always appreciated.
- *Making it clear that you care.* This is especially effective when discussing a challenge that sales prospects and their company are facing. It could be labor strife, a legal challenge, or some other situation to be dealt with. If the product or service being sold can help the situation, that's an obvious intro. But even if the client's challenge is not directly linked to the sales pitch, expressing concern and

offering good wishes that things turn out may well provide a valuable link.

3. They ask questions and take notes.

One of the biggest mistakes made by some salespeople is believing that it's up to them to do all the talking. Well, it's not. I don't have a way of measuring these things, but I fall back on the Pareto Principle and its magic 80-20 split. In business-to-business transactions, the salesperson should speak no more than 20 percent of the time. During the 80 percent of the time the customer is speaking, the salesperson should be listening, taking notes, and preparing for the next step to take.

Salespeople who start selling without asking questions are like doctors who write a prescription without asking what ails the patient. In medicine it's called malpractice. In selling it's called stupidity.

When making a first or early sales call, it's wise to obtain permission by asking, "Is it all right with you if I ask a few general questions about your company's operations?" Note the use of "general." That's a means of assuring customers that no corporate or processing secrets are being probed.

It's always wise to start broadly, narrowing the questions to topics related to the product or service being sold. The first question might be a request for the prospect to describe the company's business in his or her own words. Then the queries can become more specific, ideally based on information the salesperson acquired through preliminary research. Example: *Your environmental standards are very high. How do you plan to maintain or even elevate them in the future?*—assuming that the product being sold has some connection with environmental protection.

Questions should be specific and *open-ended*—that is, they

cannot be answered by a simple yes or no but with a complete sentence that conveys important information. The information gathered from open-ended questions should provide something I like to call *nourishment*. In a sales situation, nourishment is information used to keep things going forward, provide insight and data, and help move toward closing the sale. Admittedly, some questions may cover information already in hand, and that's fine. Salespeople should never assume they have everything they need to know.

Here are examples of open-ended nourishing questions. Again, there is no hard-and-fast rule about when to use them, or even whether to use them at all. Gaining experience, paying attention, and staying focused will bring the right questions to mind at the right time.

- What is your experience with [the category of product or service being sold]?
- What qualities are you looking for in [the product or service being sold]?
- Which is the most important feature to you?
- What is your timeline for getting started with [the product or service being sold]?
- What is your budget?
- Who else will be involved in the buying decision?

During the discussion, prompts can be asked to clarify earlier answers:

- Tell me more about that.
- Can you be more specific?
- What effect did this have on you?
- Is there an example you can give me?

These questions do more than provide important information. They indicate a serious interest in assisting sales prospects in solving their problems.

Nothing is more important to successful selling than asking questions—the *right* questions in the *right* order with the *right* emphasis. Here are rules I encourage my sales staff to follow, along with suggested phrasing:

Obtain permission.	*Do you mind if I ask a couple of questions?*
Begin broadly.	*Please tell me a little about your company.*
Build on responses.	*You mentioned you had a problem. What was it?*
Keep things simple.	*How do you feel about this approach?*
Follow a sequence.	*I understand the problem. What happened next?*
Be nonthreatening.	*May I ask how you dealt with the issue?*
Emphasize benefits.	*What would you most like to see happen?*

4. They make the experience enjoyable for both sides.

This is a vital element in all sales presentations I make. Weeks after attending a sales presentation, prospects remember few if any specs and details about the product or service being sold. But they will easily remember the mood of the meeting. "That was a fun session," they will recall. "I enjoyed the time it took to attend it." Buying decisions are made as much by the heart as by the mind, and where possible it is essential to create a positive, even "fun" atmosphere in sales presentations.

I didn't need confirmation of this view, but my years on *Shark Tank* have underlined the importance of making your presentation memorable and entertaining. All the people who succeed in having their pitch to us aired on television have one thing in common: they are not boring. They can be amusing, outlandish, glamorous, loud, overweight, underfed, or have almost any other characteristic you can name, but boring is out. Everyone remembers fun and excitement but no one remembers boring, and the last thing a salesperson wants to be with a sales prospect is forgotten. Boring is death on television, and it's definitely not healthy for sales presentations.

Silly hats and amusing stories are not what it takes to make a presentation fun and engaging. The key is to focus on making customers feel that the time spent was not wasted; that the event was a meeting of friends more than a get-together of businesspeople; that their attention didn't wander from the sales message, because both the message and the salesperson avoided boring them; and that they will look forward to attending a similar presentation in the future.

5. They may consider a Zen approach.

This could be an effective way to achieve all of the previous four steps in one move. It could even prove helpful in staying focused and in searching for ways to make the pitch an enjoyable experience. But I suspect it is not for everyone.

"Zen" does not mean the salesperson assumes the lotus position with eyes closed while meditating. I'm talking about the wider version of the ancient Eastern approach, the one designed to help people "get out of their own way."

Using the Zen approach to playing tennis, for example, assumes that the player's body knows all the basic techniques needed to hit the ball accurately and has played often enough to experience the sensation when the ball is struck cleanly and goes exactly where the player wants it. In other words, the player is at the level where the feet "know" where to be when the ball is struck, and the arm and hand "know" how to hold the racquet and when to swing it. Problems occur when the player consciously "tells" the body what to do while the ball is on its way across the net. That's when they "get in your own way." Another way of describing it: they overthink the problem at a time when they should be trusting their instinct.

Zen solves this problem by occupying the mind with something that has no connection to striking the ball. One method suggests counting the seams on the tennis ball as it flies over the net toward the player. That's impossible, of course. But by keeping the mind occupied this way, the feet and arm can do what they already know how to do.

Believers in Zen also buy into the idea that doing anything for the right reason is more important than doing a right thing for the wrong reason. That's a link here with Karma, which believes that all the good and selfless actions we make will eventually generate good and selfless responses. According to Karma, treating clients, coworkers, friends, family, and complete strangers with the same respect you want from them will reward you in a similar manner. This sounds to me like a good way to build relationships with customers.

According to those who believe in Zen as a sales technique, putting the customer's well-being before the salesperson's will lead to success. When you see it from that angle, the Zen approach sounds very much like points I have made throughout this book.

Seven Characteristics of a
Good Salesperson

1. *Attitude*—dedicated to assisting the customer first.
2. *Confidence*—believes in themselves while keeping their ego in check.
3. *Curiosity*—approaches every selling situation with their mind open, prepared to learn something new.
4. *Discipline*—ready to work toward meeting the customer's needs.
5. *Focus*—never loses sight of the twin goals of satisfying the customer and making a sale.
6. *Honesty*—recognizes the need to forge relationships built on trust while knowing that trust can be easily shattered by deceit.
7. *Knowledge*—takes time to understand all aspects of the product or service being sold.

FIFTEEN

Sometimes the Most Difficult Person to Be Is Yourself

Take this one to the bank: *the best salespeople find a way to build trust with their customers.*

Building trust leads to building solid relationships, and good relationships are vital to making sales. They are also vital, unless you choose to be a perpetually reclusive hermit, when it comes to getting along with people you care about and who care about you. This, of course, is one more time for me to point out how so many techniques used in sales are nearly identical to the way we build and maintain a social life. Not to mention a marriage.

The best way to build trust with someone is by being totally natural and free of pretension and phoniness. In other words, by just being yourself. This can be difficult for some people to do. Many things in our modern culture seem to contradict the concept. We live in a world where cosmetic surgery is as commonplace for some people as visiting a dentist, pharmaceuticals alter our behavior, and much of our social interactions aren't direct and personal—they're Facebook to Facebook. All of this makes it a challenge to say "I will relax and just be myself" and follow through on it.

Everyone has a wishful identity not because they need it necessarily, but because it is so easy to obtain. Some athletes depend more on steroids and stimulants to win medals than on their physical qualities, abilities, and training. Celebrities spin fictional histories and promote them as bestselling memoirs. Digital photography permits everyone to alter their appearance to look more like George Clooney or Jennifer Aniston than whoever they really are. And speed dating becomes more appealing than getting to know someone over a leisurely dinner.

Who is honestly real these days? It's a challenge to decide.

The challenge becomes difficult for some people who choose sales as a career. Their temptation is to look for ways to impress the customer immediately. Which may be a fine goal, but a terrible tactic.

We can all take action to create a good first impression with strangers. Dressing appropriately is obvious. So are good grooming, politeness, and a firm handshake. Beyond these basics, the next stage should be easy. Except that it's often difficult because it depends on you being *you*.

In building relationships with customers, with friends, and absolutely with life partners, none of us should be anyone except ourself. Trying to be someone we are not—more extroverted, more intellectual, more entertaining—is a recipe for disaster.

Humans are naturally intuitive. We became that way when our Stone Age ancestors ventured out of their caves in search of food, knowing that unless they were constantly aware of their surroundings, *they* could become dinner for saber-toothed tigers, crocodiles, or some other predator.

Those intuitive genes remain within us. Sometimes they set

off sirens, red lights, and other alarms in our minds when we meet someone whom we suspect threatens us. At other times the genes are subtler, saying, "There's just something about her that I can't stand" or, conversely, "I like this guy!"

Our genes respond to authenticity—the sense that what we see (and hear) from the other person is both real and sincere. Even when the authenticity falls short of perfection (as though any of us is perfect), within reason we tend to prefer authentic flaws over false perfection. Babies and puppies prove this theory.

Why does the sight a baby, puppy, or kitten create a soft and compassionate response? Because everything about them is authentic. Including the fact that they are wholly self-centered. Babies cry when they are hungry and scream when their diaper needs changing. They don't care where they are or what time it is. They demand the attention they need. We know the trouble puppies and kittens can get into, yet they create similar responses in most people.

Part of this response grows out of our understanding that young creatures need care and protection. But that's still linked to the fact that babies and other young creatures are perfectly natural in their behavior.

One of the things I enjoyed about appearing on *Dancing with the Stars* was learning the viewer response to my behavior on the show. Whenever I knew the cameras were on me, I could have been cool and acted as though it were all a walk in the park. But I didn't. I was pumped just to be there, and fascinated by the talent I saw around me. The young boy inside me kept showing himself with "Gee whiz!" enthusiasm. It was the real me, at a time when I needed to be just that—the real Robert Herjavec being himself and forgetting about the emotional pain he had been enduring for months. I didn't plan it that way, but I'm sure this won us votes from the audience.

Who might I have pretended to be if I thought it could have earned us votes? I have no idea. All my years in business have convinced me that you don't lose anything by being natural, and you risk everything by being perceived as a fake. But it still happens, especially among novice salespeople making a major sales pitch. They begin asking themselves, What if I screw this up?, What if he/she doesn't like me?, What if I say the wrong thing, do the wrong thing, ask the wrong thing?

It's all associated with wanting the other person to approve of and like us. We fear they won't, so we try to be someone else with empty boasting or by attempting to change our personality. If we are successful (and the odds are against it), it won't be *us* they like and approve; it will be the person we are pretending to be. If we go back to the example of successful selling being like performing onstage, the stress we are feeling in situations like these is stage fright. But that's where the analogy ends. As an actor, it's okay to assume a fictional identity—in fact, it's part of the job. As a salesperson, it's disastrous.

Psychologists, who rarely worry about making a sales quota, have their own reasons for encouraging us to remain true to ourselves. Authenticity, they suggest, is linked to psychological well-being. If you are truly comfortable with who you are—not necessarily what you have achieved in life, but the values and standards that define you—your self-esteem is high and you can cope with most of life's challenges.

You don't have to be a clinical psychologist to understand how that works. Trying to be someone you are not—someone you *think* the other person wants you to be—takes a lot of effort. For salespeople, that effort should be applied to making sales presentations more effective.

I know of at least four benefits that salespeople can enjoy when they refuse to don some other persona and learn to be themselves. They are also four benefits for someone who wants to sail through life enjoying as much happiness and self-satisfaction as possible, whatever career they choose:

1. They are more relaxed.

It doesn't take excess energy to be yourself. You're not busy judging how you behave and trying to see yourself through someone else's eyes. You are comfortable in your own skin, responding from the heart. One of the best ways to help others around you relax is to feel relaxed yourself.

2. They avoid being manipulative.

I hate being manipulated, or being in the presence of someone who is trying to manipulate me. I expect you do as well. Anyone who tries to choose his or her image by being someone they are not risks creating an entirely opposite effect—others will think less, not more, of them. That's not helpful. Most people welcome those who are straightforward about themselves, even if they don't entirely agree with or totally admire the other person. We cannot expect others to respect us if we do not respect ourselves, and that includes accepting who we are.

3. They listen better.

No quality is more important in successful selling than the ability to listen carefully and understand what the customer is and is not saying. Being busy creating some artificial identity while the customer is speaking means we're not listening. The less we listen, the less we sell.

4. They become more likable.

We all want to be liked, in or out of a sales situation. But face it—with more than seven billion people on the planet, not everyone in the world will admire us. Even Mother Teresa, after all, had her detractors. Once we get over the fallacy that we can make ourselves likable to everyone in the world, it becomes easier to be just plain us. Those who enjoy our company value the fact that we are genuine and that we avoid pretension and posturing.

Earlier in this book, I pointed out that almost every skill learned as a salesperson can bring satisfaction in life generally. That's because successful selling is all about relationships, and the more successful we are at developing and maintaining relationships, the happier we will be in life. It follows that we will be better in sales situations. Nothing is more important to our lives and our careers than learning to be ourselves. And the biggest barrier to reaching that goal is our own inhibitions.

We are all inhibited in various ways. Some are actually necessary, like the one that keeps us from ramming our car into the back end of the vehicle that just cut us off on the highway. Or prevents us from tossing the nearest thing at hand—a lamp, a dinner plate, a knife—at our partner in the middle of a quarrel.

Other inhibitions are subtle and limiting. They developed as side effects to our roles as social animals. The inhibitions we feel in those situations represent our need to fit in with members of our social group. "Fitting in" means being accepted by others, and being accepted suggests that we become as much like others as possible in appearance, in values, and in social measures generally. That's when we model ourselves according to the qualities of other people, which is what prevents us from being ourselves. To put it bluntly, we *fear* being ourselves.

"Fear" is a powerful word. If it need be said, it is also a very powerful emotion.

All our inhibitions are based on fear, and here's an effect of fear that no one can doubt:

Fear makes us stupid.

Remember the story of our Stone Age ancestors who left their caves in search of dinner and risked becoming dinner themselves if they encountered a large predator? They developed a protective sense that has carried down to us through all those thousands of years. It's *fight or flight,* and it describes the options that cavemen had when faced with a serious threat to their lives by other creatures. Including other cavemen.

Fight or flight means they could either stand their ground to battle the menace, or turn tail and hope to outrun it. Their only other option would be the deer-in-the-headlights response we know today. When this overtakes us and we can neither fight nor flee, we are struck dumb and freeze up. We don't know what to do because we no longer have the options that evolution created for us, and neither logic nor intelligence can replace them. Now it's either fight, flight, or freeze.

Our ancestors wandering in search of food knew the cause of their fear. Something would slither down a tree, or leap out of the water, or emerge from behind a bush with the intent of attacking them. None of these events is likely to happen these days.

We may be out of our social element at times, but this doesn't always mean our lives are at risk. Yet the same instinct applies, and when we lack guidance on how to act, we freeze.

The best way of dealing with inhibition is to understand that it is fear-based. Whenever you feel inhibited in a social or selling situation, ask yourself what you fear most. It's likely not being gobbled by a crocodile. It's probably that thing about not "fitting in," which, in a sales situation, translates into not being able to establish a relationship and thus not making the sale.

Our inhibitions grow out of the dark corners of our personality that make us insecure. Overcoming them is the key to being accepted and avoiding the fight/flight/freeze response.

If you feel inhibited about meeting a group of strangers, the fear is probably linked to one or more of these reactions:

> *You feel shy*—the overall emotional response to the fear of not fitting in. Shyness is linked to the fear of rejection; if you fail to fit in with others, they will reject you.
>
> *You have trouble communicating*—you don't know what to talk about, or how to explain your thoughts and feelings to others.
>
> *You fear loss of control*—what will happen if the conversation goes in a direction you are not familiar with, or deals with subjects you either don't understand or prefer not to discuss?
>
> *You lack empathy*—sharing feelings expressed by members of the group is impossible because you can't relate to them.
>
> *You can't express your emotions*—you stand like a stone, creating a similar response from those around you.

You feel inadequate—everyone else appears smarter, wittier, and generally more assured than you.

You have low levels of self-confidence and self-esteem—the people around you could not possibly find you interesting and entertaining.

To take these ideas a little farther down the road, consider this:

All fear-based social inhibitions are based on conjecture.

When meeting a group of strangers in a social or selling situation, our fears appear because we are worrying about what other people are thinking about us. In our fear, we may *imagine* their opinion of us, but there is no way to *know* what they are thinking. We don't have that information unless we are mind readers. If that's the case, this book should be more about getting work in a Las Vegas lounge than selling.

I don't want to make light of being inhibited in a social setting, because it may well represent or become a serious mental health problem. Painfully shy people may suffer from anthropophobia—literally, fear of people—often connected with some childhood trauma, and need professional treatment.

The majority of us do not suffer from such an ailment. We just find ourselves facing a fear that we cannot handle because we don't know the source.

Fear-based inhibitions become like habits, meaning that we react to them in the same way in similar situations. But habits, like almost all behaviors, can be changed. If we can understand and acknowledge the basis of the fears that inhibit us, and remind ourselves that we are only imagining what other people are thinking, we can set aside our initial inhibitions.

Free of those inhibitions, we can be ourselves and reverse the downward curve that tracks our declining confidence. Being ourselves creates confidence in us and in the people around us. When we are true to ourselves and confident in our actions, little else about us matters.

So how do good salespeople ensure that they are being themselves in a high-pressure sales situation? After talking to salespeople I admire, including several on my own sales staff, I identified five ways by which they deal with the issue in a selling situation.

They begin by thinking about their values and standards and how they want to live. Assessing their merits while accepting their faults leads to an open and honest attitude that others instinctively recognize. It may be "I can't be spontaneously amusing in the middle of my presentation" or "I know how to demonstrate the two most important benefits with a lot of conviction." The abilities or inabilities by themselves are not important; total honesty with themselves is.

They also pay attention to what is happening around them, not within them. Reacting naturally to whatever they see or hear, they don't overanalyze what others are saying or how they are acting.

Here's another trick: they also forget about aiming to please. This sounds a little illogical, perhaps, but it is the basis of being natural and genuine. If they have to "aim," they are not presenting themselves honestly. For example, being courteous to others is important, but the courtesy should grow from within, not be a tool to make people accept you. There is a clear difference between being courteous and being obsequious.

Worrying about how others see them—*Am I being too aggressive? Does she like my tone of voice?*—is not something they worry about. The most important thing they want others to know is that they are honest and authentic. Everything else is beyond their control—you can't be someone you are not and still be genuine—and probably irrelevant.

I know at least one salesman who repeats like a mantra, *Other people's opinions of me are none of my business.*

Does being true to themselves and true *about* themselves guarantee success in selling? It takes more than that. But on the way toward a successful sale, they can set aside one barrier to completing a sale that many people feel cannot be overcome.

Like so many other aspects of successful selling, being true to yourself can assist you in various corners of life. We are all inhibited by a vast range of influences, from family and friends to fashion and social media. Learning to be ourselves sounds foolish on the surface—do babies and kittens "learn" to be themselves?—but it can be challenging for many people. If this includes you, here are a few measures of your level of self-consciousness. You might ask yourself how many of them fail to apply to you and what you can do about it:

Seven Signs You Are Being True to Yourself

1. You feel comfortable in your own skin.
2. You feel no need to impress anyone about anything.
3. You have no problem concentrating on what needs to be done in both your private life and professional career.
4. You manage personal situations honestly and openly, without lies or exaggeration.

5. Your inner voice is quiet when you are with others whose company you enjoy and value.

6. Your muscles are relaxed and you breathe easily and normally.

7. You feel good—about yourself, about your life, about all you have achieved and all the things you plan to achieve.

I'll leave the last word on this topic to something Oscar Wilde is reputed to have said. Oscar was never anyone else but himself. This made him less appealing to some people than he might have preferred, but Oscar didn't care. It was more important for him to be himself than to try to become the person others might want him to be. Anyway, the thought, whether spoken by him or someone else, makes my point:

Be yourself. Everyone else is taken.

SIXTEEN

The Closing Conundrum: People Want to Buy; They Don't Want to Be Sold

If you haven't seen the 1992 movie *Glengarry Glen Ross* and plan to, get ready to install a filter in your mind that keeps reminding you, "This isn't necessarily real life!"

By one measure it's an outstanding movie, based on a Pulitzer Prize–winning play by David Mamet. Much of its success is thanks to a stellar cast: Al Pacino, Alec Baldwin, Jack Lemmon, Kevin Spacey, and Alan Arkin. Four of the characters are real estate salesmen (*Glengarry Glen Ross* refers to the housing developments being sold) facing a weird carrot-and-stick sales incentive. The best salesman of the month wins a new Cadillac. The second-best salesman wins a set of steak knives. The remaining two are fired. If you are prepared for its rough language and sometimes startling plot developments, it is a movie worth watching.

But it has nothing to do with modern sales techniques.

The salesmen in the movie are desperate and harassed, driven by fear and intimidated by the outrageous demands of their employer. Nothing, the sales manager suggests, should get in the way of making a sale. How the salesmen make the sale is left up to them. The only guidance provided is the ABC of selling constantly repeated by the scathing Alec Baldwin character: *always be closing.*

This phrase has been a popular mantra among sales trainers and managers for years. At its heart, it means salespeople must find a way to convince the customer to make the purchase from the moment they meet. Never mind building relationships, discovering needs and wants, handling objectives, and all of that. Everything, the theory goes, depends on finding a way to close the deal.

Dozens of books have been written and hundreds of video presentations produced, all of them dealing exclusively with teaching salespeople how to close. Many books are crammed with phrases to be memorized and delivered to the prospect at an appropriate time, over and over if necessary. "Do this," the books and videos lecture, "and you make the sale. Fail to do it, and the sale is lost."

I have a problem with that, and it has nothing to do with rules and suggestions for successful selling—hey, I've included a few of my own so far. My biggest problem is something I mentioned earlier: salespeople are not selling to robots; they are selling to people with many concerns on their mind, some related to the product being sold and others that we cannot begin to imagine.

Each prospect is a unique individual who sees the salesperson and whatever they are selling in a unique way. Standard closing lines supposedly are like hot buttons to be pressed whenever the salesperson hears clues such as "Does this come in silver?" or "How would you ship this to us?" These lines may in fact indicate a level of interest by the buyer, but responding to them with a memorized, preprogrammed line guarantees nothing unless proper groundwork has been set, including building a reasonable level of trust.

Here's another problem:

Customers prefer to buy from people they can relate to and trust. The best method of doing this is through conversation—exchanging comments and observations not directly linked to the sales process. This involves a little footwork, I admit. Both sides know their role; one is hoping to make a sale, and the other is considering making a purchase. The discussion shared about the weather or a concert that one of them attended has little to do with the product being sold and considered. It's about a personal connection being forged with the customer. Even when reviewing the product's applications, benefits, and other qualities, the exchange should reflect the relationship between both sides.

I'm not questioning the need for salespeople to nudge a prospective customer toward a decision. I'm just not happy about oversimplifying the process with an ABC line, assuming that's all that is involved. If the sale involves a complex product and an equally complex deal along with a substantial investment by the buyer, it's never that easy. Dropping a closing line into the conversation early and abruptly risks derailing the entire sales process, including everything that may have been accomplished to that point. If I may use another dance analogy, jumping to a closing line too early is like ending the music in the middle of a samba. Feet stop moving, hips stop swinging, and fingers stop snapping. The dance has ended long before it should have been over.

It's an unbalanced situation. As a salesperson, your sole expectation after delivering a closing line is to hear the customer respond by agreeing to hand over cash, a credit card, or a purchase order. But the customer may have other options. Some may be objections to be dealt with—the price is too high, the color is wrong, approval is needed from other departments, and on and on. There are ways to restore the balance, but the route to getting back after firing a closing line can be a rocky road. You can throw things off balance by trying to close too early, and risk damaging the relationship, however brief it might have been.

This is why I say that closing a sale is more complex than the how-to books suggest. Yes, salespeople need to take the initiative, and yes, they have to be exact with their timing. But there is not yet nor will there ever be a push-button solution to closing, or any other aspect of professional selling.

Here is my approach to closing a sale:

I remind myself that clients and customers buy the salesperson as much as they buy the product. My salespeople and I know more about our product, its design, and its application than the people who may buy it. Customers expect this, and they need to feel comfortable about reaching their decision by trusting the salesperson to act in their best interests.

I avoid using an abrupt closing line that can damage the comfort level I've worked hard to establish. Closing soon—or trying to—shifts the conversation from the *relationship* to the *transaction*. When this happens, things become seller-centered instead of buyer-centered, which is not a direction either the customer or I may want to go.

I reject the idea of using memorized closing lines. They include, *When can I arrange shipment to you? Would you like that in red or gray? Is there anything preventing you from making your decision now?* Comments like these assume that the sales transaction is all about me, the seller; that the buyer's decision will be entirely rational; and that a straight line can be drawn from introducing myself to watching the client sign the contract. But that's not true. The transaction should be about the buyer more than the seller, and a straight line may be the shortest distance between two points, but it's not always a successful route to closing a sale.

I take care to avoid getting ahead of the customer, because it can be fatal to an otherwise good sales story. This is all about timing. As I pointed out earlier, it's critical to remember that salespeople are more familiar with the product and its features and benefits. Customers normally are not as well acquainted and may take more time to reach the level of comfort needed to make a decision. If one of my salespeople or I deliver an abrupt closing line (*Can I write up the order now?*) too soon in the process, the customer feels rushed, and much of the rapport I've built to that point may vanish.

I take pride in my selling skill and remind myself that, like all skills, it takes ability and experience to do correctly. I don't want my closing move to make prospects feel uncomfortable or pressured. It should make them feel that the relationship we've built is developing naturally. That's more difficult than it may appear, especially for new and inexperienced salespeople, because it can trigger rejection, and no one enjoys being rejected.

In reality, a sale is not really closed until money changes hands. A purchase order or some other document from a company buying the product or service is fine, but they are not as fixed and final as a credit card or cash being handed across the counter, or a confirmed deposit in the seller's account.

I mention this because many viewers of *Shark Tank* assume that the handshake exchanged between the Sharks and successful pitchers on the show marks a closing of sorts. It doesn't. Every agreement we make with people seeking an investment from us is subject to review. If due diligence on our part exposes some stretching of the truth or outright lies by the pitcher, the deal is off.

Whenever a deal falls apart, it's usually the result of widely exaggerated sales and profit figures tossed at us during the pitch. We're a little forgiving if the truth has been stretched somewhat, assuming the balance of the story we heard was solid. But in some cases the claims of sales made and profits earned have stretched our trust and insulted our intelligence. Other deal killers are failing to tell us about partners and not having copyright or patent protection on a product.

The next time you watch a Shark shake hands with a new partner on the show, hold your assumption that both sides will be watching their wealth expand in the coming months. Yes, money can be made from such deals, but not until the deals are closed with confirmation of the claims made by the pitcher.

Few things in business give me greater pleasure than closing a challenging sale. How could it not be both fun and satisfying? Making a sale is what it's all about, and it can be rewarding beyond the commission earned.

This suggests yet another off-the-wall analogy between life and selling: *being a skilled salesperson is like being a good parent.* You can read all the child-rearing books you wish and listen to all the child psychologists you encounter, but in the end being a good parent comes down to knowing your own child and using your instincts to reach the goal you had in mind. If you do this over and over, creating good feelings for both you and your kids, congratulations. And if you can move from a first introduction through a complex sales presentation that involves building a relationship and dealing with buyer concerns and complete a sale that benefits both people, you can appreciate the connection.

Having said all of that, I agree with the original thought: being successful in sales means knowing how to close. Closing a sale is a salesperson's raison d'être. They don't want to walk away with either a promise (*I'll think about it*) or a rejection. They want to leave with a sales slip, a purchase order, or a contract in their hand, and it's up to them to get it.

How do they do this without derailing the conversation?

Instead of "stopping the music" with an abrupt request for the order, they *change* the music by asking a question such as *What happens next?*

This takes the chore of moving toward a decision out of the salesperson's hands and puts it in the hands of the buyer. It is also an open-ended question (It can't be answered with a simple yes or no), and it doesn't stop the music of the conversation. Answers to this kind of question cannot be predicted, so the salesperson can't be ready with a prepared response. They need to listen closely for replies such as:

> *We'll have to submit it to the [name] group.*
> *I could schedule another meeting with the [name] committee.*
> *Maybe I should look around a little more.*
> *I would need more data/more detailed pricing/performance figures, etc.*
> *It sounds like the same thing we've been looking at from other sources.*
> *I'm still not sure of the benefits to us.*

They may also hear the dreaded *Sorry, not interested.* That's not good news, but it moves the process forward and avoids more wasted time.

Depending on what the salesperson hears (and they should ask for clarification if unsure of the customer's position—*Sorry, I'm not sure I understand that point. Could you explain it to me please?*)—they should follow up with another question:

> *How does that process work?*
> *How involved are you with that group?*
> *When would the decision be made?*
> *Out of everything you have seen from the other companies, can you identify any differences in price, performance, or service?*
> *What would you like to see happen?*
> *What is the biggest thing standing in the way?*

Think about what they are doing here—*they are asking the prospect for help.* It's one of the most important steps to take in closing a sale, and it almost always is effective. Most people, dealing with someone whose presence they have enjoyed for even a few minutes (it's the relationship factor) are willing to offer assistance if all it takes is some words of advice.

This technique turns the closing situation back to the buyer instead of unleashing a let's-get-it-done-now line from the salesperson. The response to *What happens next?* should steer things to another open-ended question (*When would that decision be made?*). Notice that no massive leap is taking place—just a series of small steps. Objections encountered along the way are likely to be smaller and easier to handle when the closing process is handled this way.

Finally, one of the easiest to grasp but—for some people—difficult to execute rules in sales: when the salesperson finally feels that a closing question is in order and he or she delivers, they should *shut up* and not say another word until the customer responds. Silence is provocative. It encourages both sides to reflect on what has been said and what the next move will be.

This can be a challenge to some salespeople. Customers may seem to take an eternity to speak at this point in a sales pitch. It's probably just a few seconds, but when a major sale hangs in the balance, salespeople may feel their hair turning gray. It's tempting for them to fill the silence with their own voice, but it's a mistake to try. I have seen more than one customer talked out of a sale when the salesperson did not know enough to simply wait and listen. Why? Because they failed to understand the power of silence.

Regular *Shark Tank* viewers encounter this application of silence by us, and it may make them uncomfortable. More important, it makes the pitcher uncomfortable, which is often the whole idea.

One of the most feared events on network television is "dead air," when nothing happens and no one speaks. Producers and directors try to avoid dead air because they are always aware that millions of viewers are out there somewhere saying silently, "Entertain us or we'll switch channels or go to the kitchen for a coffee." Even a few seconds of no motion, no voice, and no music from the television may seem like a major error, an amateur mistake on a major network show.

On *Shark Tank,* it's not a mistake. It's a means of generating drama and tension and of moving the story forward. For just a few moments—although on network TV, two or three seconds in which nothing happens can seem like half a day—none of us Sharks speaks. We simply look at the pitcher in silence, without expression.

The frozen silence usually occurs after a pitcher has been carried away with his or her deal, spewing unrealistic events or promises that are so outrageous they appear to leave us literally speechless. (It takes a lot to make Mark Cuban speechless, but hey, sometimes it happens.) When the pitchers finally stop talking, we say nothing. We simply stare blankly back and wait for them to speak. Their expression is usually "Somebody say something!," but we don't. We sit in silence, and we watch and listen. Mostly we listen. The result is an instant of drama and theatricality.

Whatever the presenter finally says, the words will be either dramatic—"Hey, don't you guys get this??!!"—or informative, usually coming from a new direction. Both move things along and add to the show's entertainment value.

Are we being cruel and manipulative to the presenters? Not at all. We are, in a manner of speaking, providing them with the opportunity to own the time and space. The way they choose to fill it is up to them. It is admittedly a little theatrical in its impact, but that's within the context of a popular television show. In other instances and other applications, such as selling, what we are doing is immensely powerful.

People in both personal and business relationships are too often either not aware of or don't fully appreciate the power of silence. I don't mean the silence of disdain or giving someone the cold shoulder. I'm referring to the interval in a conversation when both sides are able to absorb information and arrange their thoughts before speaking.

There comes a time during a sales presentation when the next step taken by the seller should be to stop selling, which means to stop talking. At that point the salesperson's sole function is to *listen*. He or she should have been listening to the customer's response all through the pitch, of course. But at some point—and this can only be gauged with the blend of knowledge and experience built over time—the salesperson's best move is to remain silent and let the other person speak. On *Shark Tank* it's an effective moment of theater. In a sales situation it can be an effective step toward closing.

I have always been intrigued by the fact that the two words "silent" and "listen" contain the same letters differently arranged. If nothing else, knowing this is a means of reminding yourself, in whatever relationship you may be in, that the best way to listen is to remain silent.

How should salespeople deal with the sound of silence? One thing they must not do is assume they know why the customer may be taking time to respond. If they try to guess, they'll probably lose. The customer may be thinking about delivery times. If the salesperson believes that price is the stumbling block and breaks the silence by blurting out an offer of a 20 percent discount, who wins? Not the salesperson. Suddenly dropping the price when it hasn't been an issue up to that point looks like a panicky move. If the customer has been tilting to one side or the other in reaching a decision, it doesn't help to have the salesperson smelling of desperation. True, some customers may view this as an opportunity to pounce and demand a better deal than has been discussed to this point. But others will grow uncomfortable in such a situation. No one likes dealing with desperate salespeople, because desperate salespeople appear to be losers, and no one wants to be associated with losers. There is also the chance that the prospect will feel the product or service is vastly overpriced.

Remaining silent gives the customer an opportunity to object to the price, if that's a factor, and gives the salesperson an opportunity to respond. Bottom line: the price should never be reduced except in response to a request or objection from the customer.

Successful closing is indeed a selling skill, and an important one. The most successful closers, however, are the ones who control the direction of the process while letting—or even encouraging—the buyer to think it was all his or her idea.

Anyone who perfects that ability has a solid sales career ahead of him or her.

SEVENTEEN

Setting Your Moral Compass

Operating a company according to high moral standards is not only preferable—it's essential.

I need to make that point at the outset because it is impossible to expect ethical behavior from a firm's employees when the company itself is setting the bar too low.

I understand it when some people claim corporations can only become successful if they "bend the rules" here and there. In recent years we have had too many examples of large corporations not just bending rules but shattering and stomping all over them. Deciding that a corporation's welfare is more important than respecting legal limits eventually results in disaster on a number of levels. The company's reputation and its growth prospects are the first to suffer. One way or another, this leads to job losses for company employees, most of whom played no direct role in the company's misbehavior.

On a wider scale, one company's unethical conduct makes an impact on the public's perception of business ethics among other firms. The view that business is corrupt increases cynicism toward all businesspeople and the free enterprise system generally.

The fact is that the vast majority of businesses operate within the bounds of the law and widely accepted moral standards. No one notices them, of course. But everyone remembers reading about companies that become infamous for their questionable actions.

The history of business in the United States is dotted with disasters that leave many of us asking, *What were they thinking??!!* Google names such as Prudential, Tyco, WorldCom, and Enron, and you'll discover how some of the country's largest and once most admired corporations fell by the wayside. In some cases, corporate reputations were severely damaged. In others, the companies vanished completely, taking billions of dollars in capital investment and the careers of hundreds of thousands of employees with them.

All of it can be traced back to questionable actions taken by company executives—actions whose effects percolate down through managers, employees, clients, and sometimes even regulators. The collapse of Tyco, WorldCom, and Enron alone created a drop of $136 billion in market value,[1] while seventeen other companies over the same period lost an additional $100 billion. By the way, these are not just "paper losses" that do not affect you. If you invest in the stock market, rely on a managed pension plan, or count on a healthy and trustworthy U.S. business environment to fund your career, you would be affected by these kinds of actions.

Here's my point:

None of these financial disasters would have been possible if people had simply told the truth. At every level. On every occasion.

---

1. Public Citizen's Congress Watch: *Corporate Fraud & Abuse Taxes*, September 10, 2002.

*   *   *

I don't know how many people lie to me during business deal-ings. I don't believe any of them are my employees, but I can't count on it.

I balance this with the knowledge that many of the most suc-cessful people I know would not consider lying to me to close a sale. I can't speak about their personal lives, and I am not pro-posing that any of them be nominated for sainthood. I simply know—or trust deeply—that when it comes to doing business, they lock their ethical compass on north and rarely, if ever, seri-ously consider changing or ignoring it.

Why are they so serious about sticking with their ethical val-ues when making a sales pitch? A simple reason: it's good busi-ness. Being relied on to tell the truth in business dealings earns the trust and loyalty of customers and the respect of colleagues. Trust, loyalty, and respect—those are three assets you can't buy back if lost, and they cost enormous amounts of time and money to repair if broken.

Budding sales professionals are not Prudential or Enron or any of the other giant corporations that sank beneath a sea of lies. But they all depend on the trust of others to succeed. They may still risk tarnishing their reputation to earn a commission, but if they do, they jeopardize damaging their entire career.

The most respected companies and individuals I have encoun-tered in business follow strict codes of ethics. The codes vary to some degree, but they all share the values listed below. These guidelines are not infallible and, in the short term, they may not appear productive. But the wisdom of their intent cannot be questioned.

- A customer's buying decision should be based on preference, not pressure.
- The things salespeople do are much more important than the things they say.
- It is far better to compete in the marketplace by promoting your reputation than by attacking the reputation of others.
- Customers deserve and expect honest and accurate information.

Salespeople (and others—the need for high ethics is not exclusively a sales requirement) may find themselves in a position where a seemingly small lie can nudge them toward completing a sale. How do they fight the temptation to make a product claim they can't support, just to get someone's credit card in their hand or a signature on a purchase order?

I answer this with two other questions:

How much is their reputation worth? And how much would they pay to get it back?

Most people have little problem sticking to the truth in business dealings. It takes a large amount of money to persuade someone who sincerely believes in honesty to dramatically twist the truth to pocket a sales commission.

Things become complicated, however, when their boss orders them to "do what it takes" to make a sale or get some job done. The implication is clear. If doing "what it takes" involves dishonesty or outright illegality, and refusing to agree could cost their job, how should they react?

It's easy for me to advise someone to follow their ethical compass and refuse to lie to clients or customers. After all, I'm not the one who must choose between following my boss's orders and risking my job. I run my own firm, and I have insisted that my employees follow high ethical standards in place since I launched the company. Those who work for me know that if a sales situation comes down to a choice between telling the truth or telling a lie, the choice is both easy and inflexible: you always speak the truth to clients. No exceptions, no excuses.

I may lose a sale now and then by sticking to the truth, but I will not lose my job. Someone else, however, could lose his or hers by behaving that way.

So what is my advice?

Once again, it's easy for me to say, and it is both consistent and sincere:

Refuse to lie. Stick to your standards. Follow your moral compass.

In most states, employees are under no obligation to obey orders that conflict with acceptable business practices. Intentionally lying to a client or customer falls in that category, so they may be able to claim lost income if they find themselves out on the street. They can get another job. But they can't easily repair a reputation as someone who cannot be trusted.

I understand why circumstances might make it difficult for someone to defy a boss's order. They may be a single parent, for example, with obligations that are difficult to toss aside. Putting a value on their character and reputation may sound both moral and practical. But reputations are intangible; paying the rent and having food on the table each night are very real. In one case they eat, have a place to sleep, and keep their job . . . for a while. In the other, they win the ethics contest but the prize could be that they end up jobless and homeless.

My suggestion is to act from the beginning in a manner that does not encourage their boss or anyone else to consider asking them to be anything less than honest. This is far more effective than many people realize. It is possible to create an aura that deflects any suggestion of low ethical standards. And no, this doesn't mean the individual has to appear angelic or priestly. Ethics on their own do not suggest pomposity or reserve. In the workplace and among friends, making your ethical standards known reduces the chance that you will be asked to be dishonest.

I am as proud of my business success as anything I have accomplished in life. It has earned me a level of wealth and recognition that I could not dare imagine when I left university. My success also has provided well-paid employment to hundreds of talented colleagues in my companies. Together, we have achieved much for others and ourselves through the corny practices of dedication, hard work, creativity, and honesty.

When I hear of companies and individuals that believe they are entitled to similar levels of success by ignoring those practices, my response is somewhere between disappointment and outrage. Business in America in the twenty-first century has too much going for it, through innovation and productivity, to risk through dishonest and low standards of behavior. It also faces too many challenges from foreign competition and environmental concerns to tolerate corruption at any level. Those kinds of actions hurt our public image; hurt our relationship with government; and eventually hurt customers, shareholders, and employees.

If I were ever asked to offer advice to America's business leaders in fields related to consumer and investor confidence, I would say this:

Be honest in everything you do at every level in your company. No exceptions. No promises. No excuses.

Four bits of advice from me if you are asked by your boss to lie:

Say no, politely. Forget righteous indignation. Act as if you are giving it some thought, make sure you understand the request and its questionable legality, then say, "I would be very uncomfortable doing that because it sounds unethical. Sorry."

Give some thought to a compromise. There is little room for negotiation where an outright lie is involved, but there may be a way to inject honesty into the situation. For example, instead of offering a nonexistent "guarantee" to a customer as directed by your boss, ask if a "best efforts" promise can be made instead.

Look for another job. If your ethical standards and those of your employer are seriously out of sync, don't wait for the inevitable. Start looking for another job before your employer looks for someone to replace you.

Consider filing a complaint. If your boss is a middle manager in a large company, go to someone in HR about his or her request. If your refusal to be dishonest costs you your job, and no compensation is offered, consult an attorney.

EIGHTEEN

The Best Source of Your Job Security Is . . . You

I suspect most generations believe they face unique challenges in their lives. And they're correct for the most part. I don't accept, however, that the challenges we face are more disastrous than the ones faced by our parents and grandparents. As I write this, the global economic situation isn't great, but it wasn't "great" in the Great Depression, when some of our grandparents were trying to scrape by.

The world changes, and it wobbles a bit while changing. Change affects many things, including the way people make a living. Yesterday's hot careers become today's mundane occupation and tomorrow's unemployment line.

With perhaps one exception.

Despite expectations that a lot of today's occupations may vanish in the near future, I believe personal selling will be an active and critical part of business for some time yet. The emotional factor involved when customers make a purchase will remain an issue. Computer programs are good at comparing specifications, but not in every category. Many people still want to feel warm and fuzzy about their buying decisions, especially with big-ticket items.

I also believe that business is becoming more do it yourself with each passing year. The DIY movement may not have reached tsunami proportions, but many things suggest it's the future. For example, companies keep supporting the idea of key employees working at home from time to time. Many companies are also encouraging people to work "freelance," which was once translated into the term "unemployed."

Several developments drive these changes in our work habits, and I leave it for others to debate their origins and effects. It's clear to me, however, that it ties into a new free spirit that inspires people to take greater control of their lives. Many of them don't have a choice. When workers can no longer rely on trade unions or stable economic conditions to provide job security, they will look for it within themselves. If so, they may find that a successful career in selling enables them to act like dedicated entrepreneurs without being committed to working twenty-three hours a day. By setting their own work schedules and agendas, they would fit neatly into the growing DIY pattern.

This is a real possibility. The more successful they become as salespeople, the more free they are to find a way of making their sales quota. This, I need to add quickly, does not relate to retail sales as much as it does to corporate business-to-business sales. Amazon and its impact on small-ticket sales will not go away, nor will other Internet shopping services. The sales and buying process in business, however, is likely to remain for some time, whatever may happen to the press-and-purchase Amazon-based process. It's easy to purchase a book and a watch from an Internet site. It is a little more difficult to make the same kind of buying decision when spending millions of dollars on production line robotics, or hundreds of millions of dollars on a new fleet of jet aircraft.

The goal of every B2B salesperson should be to become so successful at their work that they are able to operate almost like an entrepreneur, free to plan their strategy and schedule their own time while reaping the benefits of working within a stabilized corporate environment.

American companies—not only those in Silicon Valley—are recognizing the value of employees who have a DIY attitude, especially in sales. Their approach to work enables the company to become a lean moneymaking machine, dispensing with layers of redundant personnel and complex bureaucracy.

So what does it take to reach this attractive level in corporate sales? Exceptional selling skills, for a start. Plus some personal attributes, many of them consciously fashioned. A few examples of the qualities displayed by people at this level:

- *They display self-assurance and self-reliance.* The farther people move out from under the corporate culture, the more they work without a net. This leads to an "eat what you kill" approach to their job, where their earned income is 100 percent based on their sales commissions. Some people feel uncomfortable with this idea and prefer a salary-based arrangement. Others thrive on the concept of self-reliance because they know the greater the risk, the greater the reward.

- *They possess creativity and the ability to communicate quickly and efficiently.* Choosing to work on their own may make them something of a lone wolf, but they are not the only beasts in the forest. This approach has nothing to do with the old cliché of not being a "team player." It's more like driving in a convoy down the interstate, steering your own truck in the company of others, prepared to change speed or direction when needed.

- *They understand their employer's limits and are prepared to respect them.* It's possible in a corporate sales position to take DIY too far. Good B2B salespeople remind themselves that, while out from under some of the heavier rules of a corporate structure, they still need to abide by its operational guidelines.

Some salespeople become sufficiently motivated and successful (the two go hand in hand) to convince themselves that they can launch, manage, and build their own company instead of limiting themselves to a sales role. If working as a corporate salesperson involves the talents needed to become a successful entrepreneur, why shouldn't they make the leap? It's a good question that demands a lot of sober thought.

It's true that someone with sufficient sales ability may be capable of starting their own company instead of restricting themselves to selling alone. After all, that's what I did.

My company, the Herjavec Group, is a leader in the field of providing Internet security for companies transferring large amounts of data and money among various locations in the world. Our programs and operations are complex almost beyond comprehension. They need to be, because clients assign us the task of foiling mischievous hackers, skilled thieves, and organized international gangsters. We do this with intricate multilayered programs and systems designed to identify, monitor, and deter these crimes almost before they begin.

I did not launch the company as a successful programmer or systems operator. That's neither my training nor my interest. My contributions have been, and still are, to identify a critical need, tailor an effective solution, promote the service to targeted clients, manage the sales and marketing efforts, and guide corporate growth. And it all began from the point of view of recognizing a need, sourcing the best ways to meet that need, and convincing targeted clients that we had the best possible solution—which, you'll agree, is the heart of B2B selling.

Anyone who reaches the point in his or her sales career where they believe they have the knowledge, contacts, and desire to launch their own company may give it serious thought. I can't seriously tell them to forget the idea because after all, I made it work. Such a decision deserves a book on its own. This isn't it, but here are some thoughts from a guy who learned how to do it the hard way.

THE HERJAVEC COLD-SHOWER APPROACH TO THINKING ABOUT LAUNCHING YOUR OWN BUSINESS

About 50 percent of all new companies fail in the first year. They fail for a number of reasons, including:

- *Undercapitalization*—not enough money to begin.
- *Lack of industry experience*—not knowing all you need to know at the start.
- *Lack of management experience*—not understanding the complexity of business.
- *Poor record-keeping and financial control*—not knowing where the money is going.
- *Ineffective planning*—seat-of-the-pants decision making can take you only so far.
- *Poor staffing*—your brother-in-law may not be your best choice as office manager.

- *Bad timing*—you can't be either too early or too late with your product or service.
- *Economic conditions*—jumping into a down market without the ability to take advantage of it.
- *Personal status*—youth brings energy, age brings wisdom; when do you have both in sufficient quantity?
- *Lack of supportive qualified partners*—you may not be able to do it all.

Some other things to know before launching your own business:

Entrepreneurs rarely enjoy a balanced life. The company's needs come before family birthdays, vacations, dinners, recitals, and other social events.

And then there's the challenge of multitasking. For at least the first few years of a company's existence, entrepreneurs must be at least adequate at performing a wide range of tasks, including bookkeeping, accounting, personnel management, scheduling, marketing, and perhaps a dozen other chores. They don't need to know how to perform them in detail, but they clearly need to know how to assess them. Having a competent bookkeeper is a good idea; being able to read a balance sheet and a profit-and-loss statement is essential. Failing to pay attention can lead to disaster.

Finally, it can get very lonely. Really.

I was aware of these concerns when I launched my first company, but this didn't deter me. As time passed, I was able to free myself from the demands of business to enjoy things that had not been available in the beginning. They included time to pursue hobbies such as golf and auto racing, travel with my family, and take part in *Shark Tank*.

I sold my first company to an international communications technology firm, turned another firm around from a chronic money loser to a profitable entity, and launched an entirely new company with just two employees. Today that company is a leader in its field with several hundred employees, a growing list of blue-chip clients, and a steadily growing presence in North America, the United Kingdom, and Australia.

The best measures of success for any entrepreneur are offers from other firms to buy the company he or she launched. The size of the offer marks the degree of success they have reached, especially if their company was launched with peanuts and the offers are measured in millions. I receive these kinds of offers from time to time, and it's flattering to hear the amount of money being tendered. So far I've said no, and I expect to keep saying it for some time. But whatever offer I may accept will account for the personal pride and satisfaction I have taken in my achievement.

That's priceless.

NINETEEN

Think of a Job Application as an Ad Campaign

The most important product people will ever sell is their ability to fill a job position.

And I am constantly amazed at how badly they do it.

Every day, we all sell ourselves in our roles as friend, colleague, business associate, and a dozen other relationships and exchanges. We do it with varying levels of skill and success but never think of it as selling. To us it is a means of "getting along," of presenting an identity to the world that will bring us respect, friendship, love, and sometimes business. Among the most important and clearly defined tasks of this kind is applying for a job. Many people who are quick to criticize incompetent salespeople might reflect on their own success—or lack of it—in selling their abilities to an employer.

What's the secret behind making the best possible impression when applying for a job? Here's an idea: start by looking at yourself not as a warm body ready to occupy a cubicle, but as a product or service (because you are actually both) that you are in the process of selling. Then start thinking like Don Draper on the TV series *Mad Men*.

In that show, Draper was the creative director at a large New York advertising agency, assigned to create the most effective way of selling their clients' products. If you were a fan of the show, you know he was methodical about crafting ad campaigns. He didn't toss out silly lines or emphasize cleverness over salesmanship. He learned as much as he could about the product, identified the people who represented the most likely buyers, and decided what features would attract them to purchase it. Only then would he come up with some way of persuading them through TV commercials and magazine advertisements. Draper's title may have been creative director, but he was basically a salesman.

Say what you will about advertising agencies, the people who work there are generally very smart and impressively creative. The best are also methodical about preparing campaigns on behalf of their clients, and they fine-tune their campaigns to maximize the impact. As subtle as some advertising may be, it is designed to move the audience closer to a buying decision. The audience may not be aware of the key elements in a campaign and their psychological impact, but the advertising experts always are. They know what works, and they know how to use it. Over and over.

So here's a thought:

Why can't applicants for a job use the same approach? Why can't they apply similar planning and detail to help move their name closer to a full-scale interview and, in the interview, "close the sale," so to speak?

They can.

Below are five steps that apply classic ad agency tactics when applying for a job. The steps mirror the methods used by top ad agency professionals working for clients who demand to see their sales numbers rise with every ad campaign.

To follow these steps, imagine yourself playing several roles.

First, you're the product (you're selling yourself to a potential employer); next, you're the ad agency (you'll create the campaign and run it); and finally, you are your ad agency's client (you'll earn a payoff with a job if the campaign works). The key to the campaign is the application letter you send and all the strategy and preparation behind it. I am assuming that you will be including a well-structured résumé to accompany your letter.

So forget the *Mad Men*–style cigarettes and Scotch, and never mind the skinny ties and pencil skirts. Here's how to make your job application reflect the same techniques employed by Coke, GM, McDonald's, and Clairol.

STEP 1: DEFINE YOUR TARGET AUDIENCE

Advertising professionals don't make a move until they identify whom they want to speak to about the product. Hit-and-miss targeting doesn't work. You need to know as much about your audience as you can gather. When you know them well, you will know how to reach them and what to say.

> *Don Draper asks:* Who is most likely to buy the product/service?

> *You ask yourself:* Where do I find a job doing what for whom—and what do I know about them?

An ad agency promoting a home cleaning product will look for ways to reach women primarily because, fairly or not, women in

America still perform most of the home cleaning chores. If women make most of the buying decisions where home cleaning products are concerned, why would you talk to anyone else? Advertisers reach women with commercials on TV shows watched by a larger proportion of females than males (you won't see many commercials for dishwasher soap during televised NFL games) and in magazines with dinner menus and decorating hints. Is this blatant sexism? Yes, it is. It's also the way the world works. And by the way: you won't see many power tool advertisements in *Cosmopolitan* either. You need to keep this in mind when drafting your job application.

Too many job applicants fail to take the basic step of learning who is in a position to hire them. Whatever kind of job you are applying for, always address your pitch to someone who can assess you and your qualifications. Make it as specific as possible. Don't send your application to some fuzzy title like office manager or programming department. An Internet search or telephone call can reveal the name of whoever fills that position, and a few minutes on Google may tell you their background. It could, for example, disclose that both of you attended the same college or enjoy skiing. Adding this information in a subtle manner to your application letter can separate you from the rest of the pack, and that's a key objective in your ad campaign.

Don't stop there. How much do you know about the company itself? Do you fully understand its products, history, major clients, competitive position, and other data? Learn about them and be prepared to discuss them if the subject comes up.

Advertising agencies spend massive amounts of money discovering everything they can about the people to whom they direct their client's sales message. They reach these people in the right place and in the right mood. Make sure you invest some time doing the same thing.

And in case it need be said, forget generic cover letters. Make an effort to tailor every application for each company you contact. Insert something that is specific to the company's industry and activity. *I am especially excited at the possibility of taking part in the kinds of environmental protection developments your firm is pioneering.* Or, *The recent article on your company in* The Wall Street Journal *has served as extra inspiration for me to build a career in your product field.* Keep it short, sincere, and relevant. Especially relevant.

When you talk to everybody, you talk to nobody.

STEP 2: CREATE YOUR OWN USP

USP stands for "unique selling proposition," which is a feature of an advertiser's product that the competition cannot match. The USP represents the primary reason for consumers to purchase the product, so it needs to be distinctive and impressive.

> *Don Draper asks:* **What USP will convince the consumer to buy this product?**

> *You ask yourself:* **What can I bring to this job that others cannot?**

Advertisers like to communicate their USP with a slogan. Disneyland calls itself "The Happiest Place on Earth," and for years

M&Ms have been reminding people that their candy "melts in your mouth, not in your hands."

Don't try to frame your USP within a slogan unless you're applying for a job as an advertising copywriter. On a job application, it's best to deliver your USP when discussing your education, your background, or some ability or experience that sets you apart from others. If you can honestly say "I am an avid swimmer, and I qualified for the all-state freestyle swim competition in my junior year" or some similar achievement, add it to your application. Achievements like this demonstrate that you have a competitive nature, and your success represents a USP.

Ideally, try to relate your USP to the business of the company itself. If their field is health care, for example, they may find it interesting that you spent your college summers working as a landscape gardener, but it won't be a compelling USP. If your mother was a registered nurse, however, and you served as a hospital volunteer for some time, this combination could become an effective USP to them. Frame it with a little advertising style, such as:

> I grew up in a home where health care was almost a daily topic, thanks to my mother's career as a registered nurse. Did this inspire me to gain experience in that field? It sure did! The six months I spent at Memorial Hospital as a volunteer were some of the most rewarding of my life.

If it fits your reality, make the most of a distinction that can't fail to produce a positive response:

I find I do my best work between 7:00 A.M. and 8:00 A.M., before everybody else gets into the office.

Insert a line like that in your résumé (but it has to be true), and you have subtly but powerfully communicated a work ethic that will make any employer sit up and take notice.

Just be sure it's true.

STEP 3: WHAT TAKEAWAY DO YOU WANT TO CREATE?

"Takeaway" is the impression your sales pitch will leave when an employer finishes reading your letter or recalls your job interview. It sums up the kind of person you are and the benefits you offer as an employee or associate.

Don Draper asks: What's the takeaway we want our target audience to have after viewing/reading our message?

You ask yourself: What is the sharpest memory I want them to have of me?

Takeaways are best expressed not in clearly defined terms (*she has a college degree and two years' experience in our business*) but in feelings and impressions. Your takeaway could be either negative or positive depending on the content of your written application or your behavior during an interview. Obviously, you want positive takeaways, such as:

- She is a positive person with a good deal of ambition and confidence.
- He seems totally up to date on all the technical aspects of the job.

- She comes across as warm and caring, open to a wide range of job options.
- He is a team player and self-starter who would not need a lot of supervision.

What you *don't* want to create is a *BLAH!* sense of who and what you are. (Remember my note that you can be almost anything on television except boring? It applies here as well.) Try to create some aspect of your identity that separates you from the pack in a positive manner. Otherwise, you're just another face in the crowd (or, in Don Draper's world, another can of peas on the shelf). You need to inject something in your pitch that at least plants this idea. I can't tell you what it is, because I don't know you—obviously. But I can give you two thoughts to build on.

First thought: you are unique. I'm going to avoid any Dr. Phil kind of homey philosophy here, but it's true. One of the core concepts of modern life is that among the seven and a half billion people on this planet, give or take, no two are precisely the same, including identical twins. It's a comforting thought at times. If you can identify some part of you that is distinctive, and communicate it in a natural manner in a letter, you won't be just a face in the crowd after all. You'll be someone in the crowd waving her arms and shouting, "Hey—over here!" Give some thought to doing this in a manner that will appeal to whomever you are addressing in your application. Which brings me to:

Second thought: amplify the quality that will most impress them. Don't lie, don't exaggerate, don't brag, and don't make promises you can't keep. Find a way to express, in the most convincing manner, the best quality you bring to the job. To make things less complex and challenging, go back to the first thought and find some facet of your personality, some aspect of your education, or some event in your personal history that you can link to the role.

Applying for a front-desk job at a resort or restaurant? You gotta love meeting people, and there could be a story about it in your background. Tell the story briefly and sincerely.

Looking for a job as a lawn care technician? Maybe, unlike other kids, you enjoyed mowing the lawn on summer Saturday mornings. That's a good USP.

Interested in a caregiver's position? Talk about the loving relationship you had with an elderly grandparent.

Complex jobs requiring college degrees and professional organization status will involve a more specific example, perhaps, but the goal remains: you want to stand out among all the other cans of peas.

This is beyond the branding approach I covered earlier. Branding is what you show everyone in the same way. Standing out from the crowd of job applicants is what you show specific people in a particular way. My best example? Kevin O'Leary.

If you've caught even one episode of *Shark Tank,* you don't need help from me in choosing adjectives to describe his personality. Words like abrasive, materialistic, harsh, pigheaded, and discourteous are not out of line where Kevin's concerned. These are the qualities Kevin knew would be assets in his performance as a Shark, so he played them up in his audition for the show. They are the real him, but that's not all there is to the man. (He is a wonderfully gifted finger-style guitar player who plays with great sensitivity, and has other talents that he avoids revealing.)

Kevin did not attempt to sell himself to *Shark Tank* as a nice guy who is polite to his elders and generally compassionate to everyone. This would not have helped him secure the job. He pulled a unique characteristic from his personality that suited the role and played it up. His takeaway for the producers: this guy could be the Darth Vader of reality television, a guy who brings three key qualities to the show: success and intelligence with a measure of intimidation. And it worked.

Once you have identified your takeaway, express it in an unusual and memorable manner. This may take some creativity, I admit. If creativity is an important part of the job—and of the USP you want to establish—some of the best examples I know about have come out of (surprise!) advertising agencies.

I know of a young woman who applied for a job as a trainee copywriter in an ad agency. She knew the agency would receive perhaps hundreds of letters and presumed that each applicant would know how to compose a persuasive letter.

She had little experience to talk about, and promoting her intelligence and perception alone would make her sound boastful and egocentric. Besides, they don't always ensure creative talent. So if she couldn't compete with a standard application letter, she wouldn't submit one. Instead, she boxed and FedExed a large inflated pink balloon to the agency. On the outside of the balloon she drew a woman's face with a felt-tip pen. Attached to it was a tag with her name, street address, e-mail address, and telephone number. A large pin was taped to a tag on the balloon. This tag said, GO AHEAD AND USE IT—YOU KNOW YOU WANT TO.

When the agency's creative director used the pin to pop the balloon "head," the balloon exploded and hundreds of small pieces of paper all labeled IDEA flew out. The young woman had established her takeaway—*This is a highly creative person with a sense of humor who is full of ideas*—and she won the job easily.

You don't need to be that creative. But you should give thought to the takeaway in your application letter.

STEP 4: USE A CALL TO ACTION

It's asking for the order. It's closing the sale. It's encouraging the target audience to take the next step. In this case, it's letting your potential employer know you are seriously interested in the job and look forward to an interview.

> *Don Draper asks:* How do we tell them about the limited-time offer / where to buy the product / our special purchase plan, etc.?

> *You ask yourself:* Where do I provide my address / telephone number / e-mail address, etc.—and how can I encourage them to contact me?

Advertiser calls to action are *Look for us in your grocer's dairy section,* or *Call us for details on this great offer,* or a similar line. It speaks directly to the prospective customer. Or, in your case, the prospective employer.

Providing a means of reaching you to schedule an interview should be a basic part of any job application, but don't use a wimpy close such as *I look forward to hearing from you at your earliest convenience.* Finish your letter with a line that communicates enthusiasm, confidence, and maybe a little urgency. Make it assertive but not aggressive—you want to sound confident, not conceited. Plant the idea in their minds with closing lines such as:

*I look forward to meeting you in person to fully express my en-
thusiasm about joining your team.*

Or:

*I am prepared to hit the ground running and assist your com-
pany in reaching and exceeding your expectations for success.*

Or:

*Thank you for giving me the opportunity to submit my interest
and qualifications in this letter. Please call me at [your telephone number] to set up an interview, when I can present them
to you in person.*

STEP 5: MAKE SURE THE PRODUCT LIVES UP TO THE PROMISE

Don Draper asks: Is the product going to match the claims
we make in the ad campaign?

You ask yourself: What's on Facebook, Twitter, that makes
me look bad? How about the message on my telephone answering app, or my e-mail address?

The advertising business is filled with tales of outstanding campaigns that failed because the campaign was better than the product it was selling. Or because important details were mishandled.
In Japan a few years ago, the ad agency for McDonald's dreamed
up a sales promotion with ten thousand preloaded USB MP3
players as awards. It was a great campaign that appealed to the
target audience. Unfortunately, the players were loaded with a vi-

rus that infected every computer they were plugged into. Guess what this did to the advertiser's image and sales?

What does this have to do with your job application?

If you submit your application or résumé online—most companies today ask for online job applications exclusively—your e-mail address is the first thing your prospective employer learns about you. You and your friends may think Barf bag@quark.com is a cool e-mail address, but what will the person considering hiring you think of it? Or how about MissGreatAss@vmail.com? Care to speculate on the kind of first impression you'll make?

Social networking lets potential employers track down the "you" that is not revealed in a cover letter and interview. Employers know (or assume) that you are putting on your best face when talking to them. But the face you show the rest of the world can reveal the "you" that you would prefer them not to know.

A survey by Microsoft revealed that 70 percent of hiring managers reject job applicants based on something they uncover about them online.[1] The material includes data on lifestyle, inappropriate photos, rants and rages against people and organizations, and other insights into the darker recesses of your character.

We all have multiple aspects to our personalities, but when I'm looking to hire someone, I'm not interested in party animals, proud slackers, college binge-drinking champions, or closet anarchists—nor, I'll almost guarantee you, are other employers.

Having several different aspects to your personality isn't the

---

1. Cecilia Kang, "70 Percent of Hiring Managers Say They Reject Job Applicants Because of Info They Find Online," *Washington Post*, January 28, 2010.

problem. Your politics may be the polar opposite of mine, but that's generally irrelevant. We live and work in a democracy, and different viewpoints among people should be expected and perhaps encouraged, if only because it suggests he or she can think for themselves. I'm not looking for someone who reflects my views perfectly; I'm looking for *a consistent tone of voice*. If your tone is always thoughtful and measured, I'll be impressed. But if it is like that when I meet you, yet on Facebook or Twitter or other social media it becomes strident, misogynist, insulting, or peppered with profanities, I'll wonder which personality is applying for the position.

You may claim the material you post among friends was not meant to be taken seriously and does not reflect the "real you." But how do I know?

Here's another hint: If you already have a job, never submit an employment application using your current work-related address. The immediate impression is that you're looking for a new job on your employer's time and using your employer's facilities, which is underhanded and unfair. Sure, everybody does it. But why broadcast the fact that you are doing it? It gives the potential employer a reason to reject your application perhaps without even opening it. Always use a personal e-mail address, one that sounds both mature and professional. If you need to open a new address just for job applications, it will probably be worth it.

A few more hints to add weight and class to your application:

- Your Facebook page, if you have one, may be your first interview. Review it and other places where you or your friends may have inserted embarrassing photos or comments. When you find them, delete them.

- Look carefully at your profile photo. If you were an advertised product—and you *are* at this point—this would be called the "product shot," the image that buyers look for when they go shopping. Make sure the photo is flattering, realistic, and up-to-date. If the picture was taken on your twenty-first birthday and you walk into the interview as a timeworn thirty-eight-year-old, the first impression to the interviewer will not be good.

- Never pull the trick of submitting someone else's photo as your own. It sounds silly, juvenile, and just plain dumb, but it happens. A Scarlett Johansson or Ryan Gosling look-alike might be flattered that you pretend you are her or him, but the reaction of people who meet you won't be flattering at all.

- Have a professional or experienced amateur photographer take your new profile picture. Make it a head-and-shoulders shot, not full-length. You're displaying your face and expression, not your shoes. Dress for the job you want. Smile naturally. Keep your head straight and your eyes open.

- Prepare properly for the telephone call you hope to receive. Delete the boring answering app that came with your phone or the silly stand-up comedian–style message that your buddy made for you. Record the greeting in your own measured voice and provide the information needed for callers to leave their message. Save comedy or drama for elsewhere. Do the same with your Web site, if you have one. Put yourself in the position of someone looking to hire a new employee. Are you impressed with the individual who appears on your own Web site? Do you find him or her impressive? Interesting? Amusing? Ridiculous?

Change whatever is needed to make a positive impression. If your reaction to this suggestion, "I may have flaws but am what I am, and the world will just have to take me that way," that's fine. McDonald's or someone else will be pleased to hire the "real you" to flip burgers.

- If you have a roommate, alert him or her to the possibility that a call may arrive from a prospective employer. Insist they answer it without their usual amusing shtick. Ideally, tell roommates not to answer at all. Use a businesslike voice mail to take the message and make a good impression.

Many of these ideas may suggest that the best way of applying for a job is to mold yourself into the kind of person an employer wants. That's not entirely true. If you become "someone else" on a job application, you are no longer the real you, and we saw the dangers of that in an earlier chapter. So don't feel as though you are fitting yourself into someone else's idea of who you should be. Alert and progressive companies—would you want to work for any other kind?—value individuals over flesh-and-blood robots.

Go back to the advertising analogy. I'm sure there are at least subtle differences among the dozens of hair shampoos I see displayed on supermarket shelves, but let's face it—they all do the same thing in similar ways. Yet I suspect that you favor one over the other when you go shopping. Why? Performance, of course. But just as important are the brand name, packaging, and other things that distinguish each from the other.

That's what you need to do with your job application.

Or you will be just another can of peas on the shelf.

TWENTY

Learn to Swim with Sharks Without Being One

Our show is titled *Shark Tank*. Not *Fish Pond* or *Splash Pool*. We are all hard-nosed businesspeople. We smile more than people expect, we tease and compliment each other when appropriate, and some of us even socialize a little out of the studio setting. Once we begin bidding on a deal or offering a critique of someone else's business decision, however, the teeth are bared and the water gets rough. But that's fine because we are all equal in our setting. Nothing Mark Cuban or Daymond John or Barbara Corcoran can say or do will intimidate me, nor can I menace them. When we express our disagreement with shouts and threats, it's all real and spontaneous but it's not personal or a career crisis—just great reality television drama.

Workplaces are different. To begin, they are asymmetrical, meaning that where two or more people are involved, one side tends to have more power and influence than the other. This isn't news, but it's a serious challenge for many people when those with greater power use it to intimidate others. Sometimes they see it as a means of advancing their careers. Sometimes it's an inherent part of their own deeply flawed personalities. And sometimes they are actually encouraged by business books and business commentators to become something that I find as unpleasant as the word used to describe them.

To put it bluntly, these books encourage ambitious people to act like assholes. The word—which I'm not comfortable using—is right there in the title of the books. It's intended to shock, and usually does. More to the point, it proposes that people not only act like the word in the title, but boast about it.

At its core, the philosophy preaches that the world consists of two kinds of people: those who don't give a damn who they hurt or stomp on to succeed; and everybody else, usually defined as losers.

Dig deeper into this kind of thinking and you discover misogyny, scorn, greed, and insensitivity among people who label themselves with that term. It all echoes the hoary old line "nice guys finish last," suggesting that the truly successful people in life are insensitive alpha males or females. Sensitivity to them, it follows, is a weakness, not a strength. Greed is as good in their eyes as it was in the eyes of Gordon Gekko. Summing it up: having a heart gets you nowhere, or so bullies believe.

When dealing with this kind of behavior, can you honestly survive by holding on to your sense of fairness and correctness? It's a key question in business today. We hear about dealing with bullying in the school yard. Who is addressing bullying in the boardroom and the general office area? And what is the real difference between being aggressive and being a bully? Mark Cuban has confessed that he wakes up every morning with the knowledge that someone, somewhere is going to try to kick his butt before the day is over. In a business sense, of course. I feel the same way, along with a need to react. When it comes to guiding our company toward greater growth and profit, I'll take whatever steps are morally, legally, and ethically acceptable, but I avoid acting like a bully either as a corporation or as an individual.

Keep in mind that I believe in the importance of creating steady growth for both companies and individuals. Nothing, not even a dandelion, grows by hiding in the shade. Your company won't grow by assuming its competitors will cut it some slack, and you won't grow within an organization by assuming that the only criterion your boss believes in is niceness.

So what do you do if you're an entrepreneur who believes in fairness, honesty, and respecting the rights of everyone around you? It can be a problem for some. By definition, entrepreneurs are prepared to take risks, always looking for new ways to get things done, and constantly reminding themselves why they are working so long and so hard. They are also aware—or had better be—that each day in the year their competitors are planning to win over some of their business, just as they're looking for ways to do the same. I buy those ideas, and I have applied them over the years, building my business from a wild idea into an international corporation. But deciding to behave brutally on a personal level isn't for me, and never has been. Being strategically ruthless, however, is more than acceptable. Sometimes it's necessary.

What's the difference? Think of Starbucks.

A generation or so ago, Starbucks was a small upstart coffee company out of Seattle and facing a challenge. The company's goal was to expand quickly and massively, preventing competitors from exploiting the company's unique business plan of serving premium-price coffee in relaxed, library-like settings. Its strategy was to place as many outlets as possible in high-traffic areas, occupying key locations before competitors caught on to the market shift. Like all real-estate decisions, the three most important aspects in choosing the places to open the outlets were location, location, and location.

Giant retail and food operations such as McDonald's spend millions of dollars searching for the best locations, basing their decisions on detailed (and costly) studies of traffic flow, utilities, access, local income levels, and more. Starbucks didn't have that kind of money at the time.

Their solution was to search for existing profitable coffee shops and open a Starbucks nearby, preferably across the street or even next door. Residents in the neighborhood who patronized the existing coffee shop suddenly discovered a new source that served richer, more consistent coffee in a wide range of flavors. Plus the service was friendly, and tables and easy chairs invited patrons to stay and chat with friends.

The strategy proved hugely successful. But was it fair? The competition didn't think so. Starbucks was an intruder, they declared, dedicated to stealing the loyalty of customers that the local coffee shop had built up over many years. Which was true, although "stealing" was not entirely accurate. Before Starbucks, most restaurant coffee in the United States was brewed by the gallon in stainless steel vats every morning. There it stayed until it was sold or tossed out at the end of the day, whichever occurred first. The Starbucks approach—make better coffee, guarantee that it's fresh, charge a premium price, and provide a comfortable environment—was a game changer. Still, the company was labeled "ruthless" for its aggressive policy.

Starbucks' move resulted in some existing coffee shops being driven out of business, but not because Starbucks undercut its competitors in price. Just the opposite, in fact—Starbucks coffee drinkers paid a premium for their caffeine hit yet believed they were getting better value from the new shop on the block.

So in the end, was it ruthless for Starbucks to displace the old competitors that way? Or just good business? I call it good business. Some companies, by their size and position in the industry, cannot avoid being judged as bullies. They're eight-hundred-pound gorillas in a small, crowded room—whenever they swing their arms or move their feet, somebody or something gets stomped on.

Every industry has its eight-hundred-pound gorilla. No matter how it acts or what it does, smaller creatures will find reasons to call it a bully. If you're in the retail hardware business, Home Depot is the giant gorilla. Try to compete with Google in almost any Internet application and prepare to be stomped on. Microsoft remains the giant monkey in computer programs, Exxon Mobil dominates much of the oil business, Wal-Mart plays the same role in retailing, and on it goes. Whatever these and similar-size companies do, someone can at least claim loss or injury from their actions. They may take their claim to court, but large and powerful companies tend to hire large and powerful law firms. Gorillas hire gorillas, and the result is often predictable.

My company is no eight-hundred-pound gorilla in our industry, so I have no concerns about my company behaving that way on that score. I am intent, however, on ensuring that bullies within my company are not tolerated at any level and by any employee.

It begins with the kind of people we prefer to hire. I don't give a damn about race, gender, religion, or any similar issue when choosing employees. The only qualities I focus on are the ability to do the job, the desire for competition and personal advancement, and a total absence of antisocial behavior, no matter how you define it.

I value those aspects of people in our company because they reflect my own core values. We all prefer having like-minded people around us, and we all benefit by building trust among ourselves, in and out of business. We build trust within our own walls, and ensure that the same level of trust spills over into our relationships with clients. Trust is lost whenever one member of a group fails to treat his or her colleagues with respect.

I'm told that clients consider our employees "nice" people. Other words like "competent," "dedicated," and "knowledgeable" pop up when I discuss our staff with clients, but I especially like "nice." And it's no accident. Along with other qualities, I'm interested in what makes an employee a basically good person. If I hire a manager who can operate effectively only by being a ruthless SOB, how can I trust him or her not to show the same attitude toward me? I can't. So I avoid people like that.

Sticking to this practice isn't easy. Sometimes I encounter a potential employee whose achievements are too impressive to ignore but who displays a "Just get 'er done" attitude that conflicts with my own. When this happens, I remind myself that compromising my business principles to hire him or her would mean compromising the person I choose to be. That's not acceptable.

My approach to business isn't rare but neither is it as widespread as I would like. I still encounter people who lie to me, either outright or indirectly, and whose agenda conflicts with my own, yet they want to work with me in some business venture. As time passes, I'm getting better at spotting these people and filtering them out.

The problem some people have in business is a fear of being too assertive, and this can prove a problem in maximizing their career prospects. To them, the concept of being "nice" means avoiding conflicts, working hard to appreciate everyone's point of view, and "get along by going along." That's understandable. But it's not the only way things need to be done.

Being "nice" is a personal goal, not a business solution. It will help people "like" you, but that's not the only quality people look for in relationships with others, whether as customer, friend, or lover. It harkens back to my earlier point that people want to feel important, and they gravitate toward others who make them feel that way.

Helping people feel important is a great way of building personal relationships and making sales.

When a boss or a coworker treats you in an abusive and disrespectful manner, your response may be to shrug off the incident and get on with your day. That's not always the best choice. Bullying hurts. It's emotionally painful, and pretending it never happened or that it had no effect on you fails to stop either the pain or the bully.

Bullying in the workplace is one of the top five reasons employees lose interest in their jobs and enthusiasm for their work. On a strictly business level, that's justification for me to eliminate bullying wherever and whenever it happens in my company. Which, I'm pleased to say, is rare.

It's not so rare elsewhere, however. Some human resources companies have attacked the problem with gusto and determination, to the point of categorizing the kind of bullies encountered at a workplace. Each of these tyrant types use different techniques but they all have the same effect on those around them . . . and they all need do be dealt with effectively.

Here's how one celebrated HR professional categorizes common workplace bullies.[1] I hope you manage to avoid countering any of them during your career, but the descriptions may sound familiar:

> *The intimidator.* Thrives on menacing words and actions to make sure their dislike of someone is both heard and felt. Uses the perceived power of their role to justify their behavior.
> *The sexist pig.* Revels in treating the opposite sex as inferior. Makes comments intended to demean other employees and lower their confidence level.
> *The scab picker.* Sees something that is a sore point for a work colleague and "picks" at it until the employee "bleeds." Focuses again and again on the same spot like a laser beam, preventing healing from taking place.
> *The screamer.* Loud, obnoxious, and abusive individual with one goal: to berate and humiliate others in public. Thrives on the notion that others fear him or her.
> *The two-faced snake in the grass.* Says one thing to your face and another behind your back. Tries to destroy reputations and takes credit for work they didn't do.

It's bad enough when bullies like these are workers at your level. It's worse when they are your boss or manager, which makes them difficult to avoid.

So what do you do? Some tips from the same source:

---

1. Ruth K. Ross, "The Dirty Little Secret Corporate America Doesn't Want Out," October 22, 2015 (http://www.ruthkross.com).

- Remind yourself that you are a target, not a victim. Seeing yourself as a victim is defeatist.
- Handle the bullying as though it's a daily job task. Be methodical in how you behave, perform as well as possible on the job, and document each incident.
- Remain calm and unemotional.
- Keep and display your self-esteem, along with a positive attitude. Do not give the bully the satisfaction of knowing how his or her actions are affecting you.
- Avoid being isolated by the bullying. Maintain connections with others around you; chat with them while avoiding direct reference to the actions of the bully and their impact on you.
- Never yell back at a bully or display any deep emotional response to the situation. Excuse yourself by saying you have a meeting to attend, a chore to complete, or you need to use the restroom.
- Start a "get out" strategy. Bullies usually do not change their behavior; it's better for you to take control over your life than expect others to change.

You can meet sharks anywhere, not just in the sea or in TV studios. Sometimes they're not true bullies like the breeds listed above, but their actions or comments can be hurtful and demeaning. Remember to speak up calmly, avoid making personal attacks on others, and be prepared to discuss whatever bothers you. This isn't just good for your personal relationships and career, it's also good for your health. Holding your frustration and anger inside will not benefit your blood pressure, digestion, or a range of other health issues.

Difficult situations, with or without the presence of a bully, may arise through disagreement about something you say or do, or an opinion you express. Face it: try as you might, you will never please everyone all of the time. No one can. Accept that fact, remind yourself that the only one you really need to please is yourself, and move on.

Sometimes the problem is deciding when and how to be assertive. Being assertive does not mean being pushy or aggressive— it means being confident enough to respond honestly, gently, and firmly in situations that offend you. Many people want to avoid confrontations, and that's understandable. But if avoiding them means you harbor anger or resentment about the situation, that's not good.

Becoming assertive can mean changing your behavior, which isn't easy, but it's always possible. If you resent the aggressive panhandler who has his hand out and you begrudge giving him a dollar, look him in the eye, wish him a nice day, and walk on. Or if someone speaks sharply to you simply because it makes them feel good, let them know it isn't necessary to use that tone of voice. The first time you do this is difficult. The second time is easier. Much easier.

When you change your behavior in these ways, you'll make some people uncomfortable. This doesn't mean they no longer like you. It means they have to adjust their reaction to you. They may ask if there is something wrong in your life. Assure them there isn't, and keep smiling.

TWENTY-ONE

It's Not the School Prom
(but Sometimes It Feels That Way)

Somebody once described adult life as "high school with money." Even as adults, many of us are subject to the same challenges and emotional crises we faced when the prom was a few weeks away and we didn't have a date. Or we hadn't been chosen to be in the big music or drama production. Or some other traumatic event in adolescence whose scars we scratch now and then, just to remind ourselves of the pain.

If your high school years were free of this kind of agony, good for you. Just accept that you escaped some important lessons in how to handle the rainy days we all encounter. Life can be wonderful and fulfilling, but it's never perfect, and there's not as much to learn from success as there is from failure. You won't win every competition you enter or have an ideal relationship with every friend and every member of your family. When you experience failure, try to remember that there is no better way to learn about yourself and about getting the most out of life than stumbling now and then.

Don't take my word for it. Bill Gates, who by any measure would be considered one of the great success stories of his generation, said, "It's fine to celebrate success, but it's more important to heed the lessons of failure."

I'm with Bill.

Mature and effective salespeople deal with failure in two steps. The first is *getting over it.* The second is *understanding what you learned.* I suspect that this counts more for salespeople than maybe any other profession.

GETTING OVER IT

When you were a child, your parents may have advised you to "get over" some personal crisis that left you feeling miserable. I doubt their advice worked, but it was probably based on similar pain they suffered in their childhood. From the perspective of maturity, they understood that the crisis wasn't nearly as traumatic as it appeared at the time. If they got over it, you can get over it. Of course, they were mature individuals at the time and you were a vulnerable adolescent, which made it difficult to accept their advice. When you're in pain, being told to "get over it" is not much help.

Rejection in life is part of growing from a child to an adult and, for novices in sales, it is part of the process of becoming a confident and successful salesperson. The only effective way for anyone to learn about his or her relationship with the rest of the world is to put themselves in positions where success is never assured; that's when they are able to judge both their response to failure and the reaction of others around them. You can eliminate threats of rejection by staying boxed within your own comfort zone, free of challenge and risk, but if that's your choice you will not only fail to grow, you will also fail to live.

So how do professional salespeople deal with losing a sale? It's easy to say they "learn" from it, although they usually do, but not all lessons need to be painful.

The first thing they need to do is put it in perspective. A lost sale is hardly a success, but that doesn't make it a personal rejection. Yet that's often the first response from novice salespeople and, depending on the situation, from experienced ones as well. There are many reasons for losing a sale, and learning what they are is where the lesson begins. Unless the salesperson knows for a fact that the loss of the sale was the direct result of something he or she did, or failed to do, they should avoid taking it personally. And if the loss *was* their fault, they should recognize that they have learned a direct if painful lesson, reducing the chance that it will happen next time.

Behaving like a professional in the face of failure is an absolute must. Phone hang-ups, head shaking, and sneers are for children. Good salespeople remain polite when informed of a lost sale in the presence of a prospective customer. They may express their disappointment (natural response); ask the reason behind the decision (a fair question); then inquire about staying in touch with the customer (wise move). I cannot count how often this mature response to a missed sale by our company has paved the way for an invitation to a future sales opportunity. Often we won the second round because we had established a relationship and perhaps corrected whatever had cost us a sale the first time. I suspect that, in a few cases, we earned that second chance because we had left the customer feeling good instead of guilty when we missed the first chance.

Dealing with the emotional response to a lost sale pays

dividends in other ways as well. Emotions are a form of energy, and when the mind becomes flooded with negative feelings released from learning that all the time and effort to make a sale failed to work, logic gets crowded out and emotional pressure begins to build. That's a natural response. When you drive yourself with passion and all your efforts fail, the passion and pressure must be released somehow. There are various ways to do it. I suggest to my staff that they write a letter to someone about their feelings but don't mail it; I tell them to set the letter aside, read it the next day, and toss it away. This often works. So does taking a walk, working out at the gym, going shopping, seeing a movie, or discussing the failure with colleagues and listening to their own experiences. In many ways it doesn't matter what they do, as long as they find a way to release the pressure and keep it from burrowing away within them.

Salespeople need to remember that the same great feeling they enjoyed when they scored a success in the past will return with their next hard-won sale. And the best way to get there is by planning their next sales pitch to a promising customer.

UNDERSTANDING WHAT YOU LEARNED

The first step for a salesperson to take after a failure is to return to the source by politely asking the customer why another product or service was chosen over the one they were selling.

This, by the way, is *not* the time for "Yes, but," as in "Yes, but we can do [this or that]," in hopes of salvaging the sale. It never works. If the "Yes, but" includes reducing the price, the customer will understandably feel the price was inflated at the beginning, which sounds suspiciously like greed. Unless the customer's understanding of the offer is seriously flawed, the train has left the station on this sale, so the salesperson needs to abandon any hope of running to catch up.

Once the key reason behind the failure is understood, the lesson learned and a description of how and why the failed sale went wrong should be recorded. With time and experience, such a record will measure the progress being made and help avoid repeating similar failures in the future.

Finally, salespeople should review their goals to ensure that they are being realistic. Some salespeople push themselves beyond reasonable limits in the sales volume they aim to achieve. I love it when my salespeople set their sights high, but they risk too many failures when they go beyond their abilities. Every failed attempt costs time, and time, remember, is not a recoverable asset. I would rather they score 75 percent success from fifty presentations than 25 percent success from a hundred presentations.

I'm not an expert on Japanese culture, but I encountered this Japanese proverb that sums up a good approach to becoming successful in business:

Fall down seven times, stand up eight.

Okay, it's very simple. Maybe insultingly so. But it's effective if you understand how it relates to several things, including persistence, courage, and believing in yourself. And the number of times doesn't matter. The concept works even if you fall down a thousand times, because each time you get back on your feet. The only way you lose, the proverb teaches, is if you fail to stand up again. As long as you are able to stand, you have hope. And as long as you have hope, you are not defeated.

This may sound idealistic at first glance. I mean, how can anybody get back on their feet after falling a thousand times?

I'll bet you did.

I'll bet that, as a toddler learning to walk, you fell many times. Maybe as many as a hundred, or even a thousand. You may have had a good cry now and then, and you may have relied on a parent to help you stand. But that's what you did—you stood up and resumed moving. Over and over. Which is how you learned to walk.

And why, when you finally got to the prom . . . you danced.

TWENTY-TWO

How to Ask for a Raise

Of all the dealings people have with their boss or manager, probably none makes them more edgy than asking for a raise. That's understandable. Everyone prefers to be sufficiently rewarded for his or her work, and everyone would like to believe that their worth is so obvious that they shouldn't have to negotiate a fair return. It sounds too much like begging. When they feel that they are insufficiently paid, they need to take action on their own. Like so many other things in life, they can do it well or they can do it poorly.

Most people do it poorly.

Failed requests for a raise are similar to failed pitches made on *Shark Tank*. No surprise there—both involve asking for money. The big difference is that employees already have a relationship with the person from whom they want money, but we know little or nothing about the people who appear on *Shark Tank*. If we turn them down, we don't expect to see them again. But if I turn down a request for a salary increase from an employee whom I generally admire and want to retain, I'm in a difficult spot. In many ways, I *want* them to make a good case for a raise, because it will confirm or maybe reveal their value to my company and make it easy for me to justify increasing their salary.

But this doesn't always happen. As on *Shark Tank,* some efforts make me roll my eyes wondering why the employee believes he or she deserves a raise and where they managed to find the nerve to ask for one. In both cases—budding entrepreneurs on *Shark Tank* and hopeful employees in my office—the same weaknesses keep appearing. Here are a few:

Poor preparation.

Getting a raise is never "Ask and ye shall receive." It's about making a sale. Which means that having good selling skills and instinct pays off in yet another way you didn't expect.

As an employee, you're not begging for alms or counting on a handout—or you shouldn't be. *You are engaged in a business negotiation,* and you should think of it in those terms. A personal relationship may exist with your boss or manager, but it is also a business negotiation like any other: she has control of money (or access to it through her supervisor), and you want a larger share of it. How do you get it? By selling your value to the company, which involves justifying the quality of your work and your performance on the job. You need to do it in the right setting, with the right tone, in the right place, and at the right time. And you need to be prepared to back up your claims.

The biggest difference between the selling skills I have been discussing and the ability to ask for a raise is the matter of relationship building. As an employee, you have, I can assume, a relationship with your boss already, so there is no need to build one. Nor is this the time to enhance or repair it. The value of the relationship is the ability for each of you to speak both casually and honestly to each other.

Time and again on *Shark Tank,* we encounter people who ask for hundreds of thousands of dollars strictly on the basis of their invention or plan. They, of course, believe they have come up with a wonderful new idea that cannot possibly fail. We don't. Not right away. We need evidence. So we ask to see sales and profit figures or inquire about the exclusive nature of their product or wonder how they plan to spend the money we are asked to hand over. If they can't provide a reasonable answer, our response usually consists of two words: *I'm out.*

Don't fall into that trap when asking for a raise. Be prepared to sell your value to your boss, with solid facts and a respectful manner.

Unreasonable expectations.

Do you honestly believe you are worth twice as much money as you're earning now? Good for you if you have high expectations; bad for your chances if you're not able to justify them.

Most companies budget about a 5 percent annual increase for salary costs. The only way to reasonably expect an increase of more than 5 percent or a raise in salary more than once a year is by being granted a major promotion. Asking for too much money without a serious effort to justify it suggests you are either out of touch with reality or greedy. Maybe both. Neither is impressive to your boss.

Lack of confidence.

You're nervous about asking for a raise? No surprise there. So are the people asking for investments from us on *Shark Tank.* We prefer not to see nervousness, either as bosses or as Sharks.

We feel more relaxed and attentive when someone making a pitch for money does it with confidence and assurance. It strengthens your case when trying to convince your boss that you deserve a raise. If you can find a way to hide your nervousness and find the balance between confidence and arrogance, you'll improve your chances of success.

Executives of successful companies agree that good employees represent their most valuable asset. These executives don't resent dealing with reasonable requests for raises as long as the employees making the requests are prepared to justify their value. Keep that idea in mind.

I can't promise that the following ten steps will ensure getting a raise every time you use them. But I can promise that they will add to your confidence and even help impress your boss.

Ten Ways to Ask for a Raise

1. Timing is important.
Don't ask for a raise during your annual performance review meeting. Unless you need to follow your employer's established schedule for raises, make your request three or four months before your review, when a raise can be budgeted according to your performance. Another hint: try asking for your raise late in the week, preferably on a Thursday or Friday. Managers tend to be more responsive just before weekends. Try to make it just after lunch, if possible. Most people feel relaxed in the early afternoon. Make it clear when you ask for a meeting that you want to discuss your remuneration level (note it's "discuss," not "ask for a

raise"). No one appreciates being blindsided with an unexpected challenge or demand.

2. Do not beg or plead.

I'm sorry if your day-care costs have gone up or your spouse lost his job or some other event has proved a disaster to your finances. That is your problem, not mine. As a manager I will listen to your tale of woe, buy you lunch, consider a loan or advance, maybe help you find credit counseling. But there should be no connection between your life challenges and the operation of the company you work for. Any assistance offered by your boss or the company you work for should be viewed as charity, not as remuneration for your work.

So don't launch your case with tales of your adversities. Start by convincing your boss that you deserve the raise. Should an opportunity to mention your personal difficulties arise in the conversation, feel free to discuss them if both of you feel comfortable about it. Just remember that you're asking for a justified raise, not corporate sympathy.

3. Add to your worth with a commitment.

Earning a raise isn't about the past; it's about the future. You are proposing that the increased salary or sales commissions you earn over the next twelve months will be more than balanced by an increase in your value to the company. Make this point effectively, and you improve your chance for more money.

Take time to consider how to upgrade your performance level. With new training? Assuming extra responsibility? It doesn't have to be a major overhaul of your duties. Just confirmation that you represent a valuable asset to the company.

4. Look for ways to gain leverage.

Try to find some aspect of your work that is valuable and unique, and be prepared to describe it. If you are the only employee qualified to perform some key aspect of the business, or are responsible for generating substantial sales or profits and your income is out of line with your contribution, don't assume that your boss is aware of it. Make sure it's known.

5. Keep the Three Ps in mind.

Practice your pitch until you know what you are going to say in response to the questions you are likely to be asked. Understand the company's *perspective* when it comes to awarding you a larger salary or commission. And be *proactive* by asking what it will take for you to earn the raise.

6. Be confident, not cocky or arrogant.

Unless you are both serious and prepared, never threaten to look elsewhere for a job if your demands are not met. Empty threats do not help your case. In fact, any threat of this kind could end your career with your employer. Whenever I hear an employee say in effect, "Match my offer or I'm going elsewhere," I know their mind is already made up to leave. And how do I respond to raises backed by a threat? I don't. Neither, I suspect, will your boss.

7. Bring proof of your performance.

Look for ways to prove that your work has improved over the past year. Suggest that your improved performance will extend into the months and years ahead, in line with the company's goals. Put the facts on paper, or use a PowerPoint presentation if necessary. A written summary of your expectations and rationale will be more than convincing to your boss; it will be helpful if he or she has to go up a level or two to get approval for your raise.

8.   Never make it personal.

You're talking business, not the unfairness of life or the perceived unfairness of your boss. Stay cool and calm while discussing your request. Remember that your manager may have to follow a corporate policy, consult with someone on a higher staff level, or do both. If you have an issue about your boss being unfair or unappreciative of your work, deal with it separately, not when you're pursuing a raise.

9.   Overcome the gender difference.

I expect managers in my company to be gender neutral when it comes to setting salaries. Women represent some of our best sales and technical leaders. They are no less assertive or aggressive than their male colleagues, and it's time we end historical stereotypes in business. There's no room left for the gender gap. If you have the ability, the attitude, the training, and the ambition to perform your job at the level your employer anticipates, your gender should never be an issue when seeking an appropriate salary level.

10. If all else fails, change may be good.

My warning about never threatening to leave your current job if your salary expectations are rejected still holds. If you are honestly convinced that refusal to deal with your salary request is unfair, perhaps it's better for you to move on. But be sure to prepare for the move and avoid making a snap decision.

Start by answering some hard questions that extend beyond your employer's refusal to grant you a raise. Was there a promise of a future promotion or salary increase? If so, how sincere do you believe it was, and how much is it worth to you? Consider the value of your relationship with work colleagues—if they represent an important part of your social life, will it be easy to give it up? Or how much are you perhaps missing in future work opportunities by staying where you don't feel valued or appreciated?

If you are thoroughly disappointed in the response to your request for a raise, give yourself the freedom to look around for other opportunities. You may discover something far more rewarding in salary and job satisfaction.

Of course, you just might find that your current situation isn't as bad as you thought.

TWENTY-THREE

If You Can't See It,
You Can't Reach It

The artist Michelangelo had amazing insight into the workings of human beings, which may have had something to do with his artistic genius. In any case, I found a quotation attributed to him that was both relevant to this book and in tune with our times. Here it is, complete with his full name (you know you're dealing with someone special when the world knows him or her by their first name alone):

> The greater danger for most of us is not that our aim is too high and we miss it, but that it is too low and we hit it.
> —*Michelangelo Buonarroti*

I've met many people who accomplished great things in business, music, and sports. None of those who reached the top of their game, from Celine Dion and her music producer David Foster, to Oprah Winfrey and UFC champion George St-Pierre, ever complained about aiming too high. But I know of others who, at the midpoint of their lives, regretted that they never realized their full potential because they were too easily satisfied. They were the ones, in Michelangelo's words, who aimed too low and hit it.

I'm not suggesting that everybody try to reach the same level of success as Oprah, or that they invest money to become as wealthy as Warren Buffett. But I believe we all inherit natural abilities that set us apart from our peers. Many of us take a long time to recognize just what those abilities are. It can happen as early as our teenage years or as late as our forties, but at some point in our lives we know what they are. From that point forward, much of our inner satisfaction derives from how we use our talents and the things we achieve with them. Not all, by the way, are material goods or passing fame.

Our lives are governed by many things beyond our control. We come up against economic, gender, and other challenges we cannot avoid because they are handed to us at birth. Many of these challenges can appear overwhelming to people who set high career goals for themselves. But they are not insurmountable. They certainly weren't to Michelle Obama or former Xerox CEO Ursula Burns or Sam's Club president and CEO Rosalind Brewer or tens of thousands of other American women who have managed to break through economic, gender, and color barriers.

It was far more difficult for these women to achieve their level of success than I can imagine, and I agree they are exceptions who prove the rule. But they broke that rule anyway, and it wasn't easy, I'm sure, which made it all the more satisfying to them. They were also told at some point, I suspect, that they were aiming too high, given their circumstances of their birth. If so, they didn't listen. Good for them.

When we arrive on this earth to begin our lives, we can't control where we land. But we can work to control where we go from that point forward, and every step we take on our own is a measure of the kind of person we are.

I'm not qualified to deal in matters of psychology, and I'm not comfortable spewing incentive slogans, so I won't go any deeper into the matter except to offer this bit of wisdom:

What you've got is what you've got.
What you do with it is who you are.

Which brings me to setting goals.

A few years ago two young guys named Nick Morton and Evan Mendelsohn heard about an annual party where people wore ugly Christmas sweaters, with reindeer, snowflakes, Santas, and assorted other tacky representations of the season. Everyone voted for the ugliest Christmas sweater, and a trophy or some other prize was awarded the winner. When these two college buddies decided to throw a similar party, they were unable to find sweaters that qualified. The best they could do was to check out ugly women's sweaters at thrift stores . . . and Christmas lights went on in their heads.

The fashion industry is always a great place for new people to make their mark, but this one was unique. Instead of competing with the likes of Ralph Lauren and Calvin Klein, Nick and Evan went in the other direction. Fashion didn't count; original ugliness did. Knowing little about running their own business and even less about the clothing industry, the two men pooled their money to launch Tipsy Elves, dedicated to the idea that a large number of people would spend money on well-made, reasonably priced, and really ugly Christmas sweaters.

It worked, to a point. The guys built their sales to about $600,000 a year. To go farther, they knew, they would need both cash and management guidance, so they beat the odds and made it to *Shark Tank*. I liked everything about Evan and Nick and their company. I liked their enthusiasm, their confidence, and the fact that they had built their business large enough to prove they had a good product and a substantial market. Sold on their future, I invested $100,000 in Tipsy Elves in exchange for some equity in the company and a role in managing the firm. In 2015 the company was on course to score about $12 million in annual sales.

It would be easy to say that Evan and Nick launched their own firm for the same reason I launched mine: they needed a job. In their case, it's not true. Evan was a corporate lawyer and Nick was a qualified endodontist. They could have coasted through their lives earning good incomes and for the most part letting other people guide their ship. Instead, they had a vision where they would have fun; take more charge of their lives and careers; do something no one else had done in quite the same way; and, with luck and sweat, make even more money from their efforts.

With goals like that and a substantial, virtually untapped market, how could I resist?

Most of us set various goals to achieve through the course of our lives. They begin with things like *Make the volleyball team* or *Get a high score on the SAT.* When we begin to accomplish the things society expects of us and we expect of ourselves, the goals become common. We seek to establish relationships, find a job, raise children, and so on. Eventually the idea of setting goals unique to us and our interests begins to fade. It shouldn't.

Whenever I hear people say they have abandoned a goal they once had, I know it's because they made at least one of these mistakes:

They didn't work hard enough.
They didn't set a realistic goal.
They didn't measure their progress and react to changing situations.

If your only goal in life at this point is to meet all of the middle-class expectations of being self-sufficient, maintaining a stable relationship, starting a family, and being a "good citizen," that's fine, of course. But I wonder whose goals you are meeting: your own or society's.

I like to think that each of us has unique abilities and expectations. If you agree, and if you intend on making as much of your years as possible, you need to set goals. Here are a few ways to get started reaching them.

Make them descriptive.

Remember when you were young and dreamed of owning a red convertible sports car, or moving to Paris and working in the fashion industry? They were perhaps more dreams than goals, but they were real to you because they were specific and you could *see* them. Make your career goals come alive the same way. Don't set a goal to make more money, or move up in your company next year; identify the amount of money you want to make, and the position you want to receive in your next promotion.

George Lucas, creator of *Star Wars* and a dozen other break-through movies, once said, "Dreams are extremely important. You can't do it unless you can imagine it."

Keep them reasonable, achievable . . . and your own.

Your career goals should be things you truly believe you will reach in a year or two. After reaching them you can set new and higher ones.

The number of goals you choose may be infinite, but the time and energy you have are limited. Forget quantity and focus on quality. I suggest you set three and no more than five. Beyond that number you don't have a plan; you have a shopping list.

One more hint: be sure the goals you set are *your* goals, not those of your partner, your family, your friends, or your boss. Others may think they know what's best for you, and their motivation may be sincere. But you can't expect to work as hard to achieve other people's goals as you will to achieve your own. Listen politely, thank them for their suggestions, give their advice some serious thought, then choose what you and you alone believe is best for you.

Ensure that your goals are positive.

Whenever I hear someone say they have a goal to lose weight, I know they have a problem. Why? Because the phrase refers to what they *don't* want—their excess weight—instead of what they *do* want, which is to become slim and healthier. That's the positive goal they need to set—not to lose weight but to get healthy.

Set a schedule.

How often have you heard someone say, "Someday I'm going to start my own company," or "Someday I'll take that sales training course and learn the skills I need"? Do you know what "someday" means? It means "*never*." If you do not set a schedule for the things you truly want to achieve, they will never happen.

Make sure your motives are strong enough to survive challenges.

Why do you want to achieve your goals? If your only answer is to make more money or drive an expensive car, rethink your plan. You are sure to encounter challenges and roadblocks to reaching your goals, and if your only motivation is driving some car or wearing expensive clothes, it will be easy to give them up.

Set milestones along the way.

Break down a goal such as "Next year at this time I will be the top salesperson in this company" into smaller steps ("I will increase my sales by half in six months"). These will measure your progress and confirm that you are moving in the right direction. And if you miss a milestone, don't shrug it off. Discover the reason and do something about it.

Make adjustments as you need them.

Surprising things will happen on the way to your goal. They may include the appearance of a new competitor, financial problems with a major customer, or a dozen other unpredictable events.

Be aware of random changes, both positive and negative, that pop up. Not all are significant or can help you reach your objectives, but some surely will. You need to know when they arrive; evaluate them; and, if it makes sense, start using them. Technological advances, for example, occur faster than ever. Stay aware of them and use the ones that promise to help advance your career.

Remember Pareto.

He's the man who discovered that 80 percent of your results come from 20 percent of your efforts. Identify and emphasize that 20 percent.

TWENTY-FOUR

Beware of the Bull's-eye
on Your Back

I **have two** connections with the rapper known as 50 Cent. The first was made when I bought a Rolls-Royce from him several years ago. The second is a comment he made in the summer of 2015, after he declared bankruptcy. Many of his financial and investment problems, he said, were caused by people who had worked to knock him down and leapfrog over him. They had been more interested, he said, in demeaning him and his success than in reaching the same kind of goals he had achieved. Then he added, "When you become successful you get a bull's-eye painted on your back."

I knew what he meant. And the bigger you get, the bigger the bull's-eye becomes.

Success breeds envy, and envy breeds other things, most of them bad. I don't know if your future success will rival 50 Cent's or mine. If it does, I'll offer my sincere congratulations and a sharp warning: as soon as you reach a level of success beyond that of colleagues within your business and personal circle, the bull's-eye that 50 Cent talked about will appear on your back. It won't be tattooed. In fact, it will be invisible to you. To others, it will be more than visible; it will become an irresistible target.

* * *

Until recently, I drove powerful and expensive cars at racetracks around the world. It was a serious sport. The cars could reach more than two hundred miles per hour, and over the four years I participated in the races I managed to win my share of them. (I also managed to crash twice, and each crash taught me something new about racing. That's the value of failure.)

I knew the other drivers I raced against, and they were all fine guys. Away from the racetrack, I enjoyed their company. We talked and laughed together about various things. During the race itself, however, things changed. They were no longer my friends, nor was I one of theirs. Now we were competitors who saw everyone else as a threat. If I approached a slower car ahead of me, it didn't matter how friendly I had been with the driver before the race began. My attitude became *Get the hell out of my way!*, which I might actually shout over the noise of the car's engine. This was a competition, damn it, and I was in it to win. So was every other driver on the track, and each of them, I'm sure, screamed the same words at me, either aloud or to themselves, when I was in front of them. We all had bull's-eyes on our backs.

Our attitudes on the track had nothing to do with envy and everything to do with being determined to win. That was the goal for each of us, and we all agreed that whatever steps we took to win would be both fair and necessary.

Envy in the workplace is neither fair nor necessary. It's unfair and destructive. It is also inevitable. If you set your goals high and meet them, you'll paint a target on your back without knowing it's there.

Don't let envy and jealousy from others deter you from aiming high in your work. There are ways of dealing with negative reactions and the office politics that go along with them.

Begin by recognizing that jealousy grows out of insecurity. People unsure of their business or personal relationships can become jealous of anyone who appears to succeed where they appear to fail. Some are able to channel envy where it belongs: as a positive force that inspires them to prove they are capable of similar success, like the race car driver screaming for me to get out of his way. Others are not so successful.

Jealousy and its effects in the workplace can dampen the good feelings you have over your success. Be warned that it can also foster gossip that could damage your relationship with your employer. Some gossip may be easy to laugh off, but should you?

As soon as you sense jealousy from a coworker, try to avoid letting it blossom into resentment. Mention some positive achievement by whoever is sounding jealous about you. Don't lay it on thick; insincerity is as easily sensed as jealousy. Say "Nice job on that XYZ account," or make some other comment that recognizes the person's qualities. Jealousy grows out of insecurity, and there's nothing like an honest compliment to make people feel better about themselves.

Avoid a negative response. Do not compare your accomplishment with theirs, and never accuse them of being jealous of you, no matter how true it may be. Tossing a negative comment at a jealous person is like throwing fuel on a smoldering fire.

When jealousy explodes into something destructive, including slandering you and sabotaging your work, stay cool. Write down the date and whatever the other person said or did to attack you and your work. Print and keep any offensive e-mails they send you, and find work colleagues who may have witnessed the jealous attitude and actions. Having a record of whatever occurred between the two of you will add credence to your position if things grow bad enough.

Some people believe that office politics are inevitable whenever bright, ambitious people are gathered in a high-pressure environment. I don't buy that. I work hard to find ways of relieving pressure and to build a healthy teamwork attitude among everyone in my company, with the goal of neutralizing or preventing office politics. It's worth all the effort we put into it.

If your company is not successful in keeping the lid on office politics, take the initiative on your own. Here are some hints that I emphasize to my staff:

Try to get along.

It's all about balance. We need to learn to be pleasant and professional, becoming assertive when necessary. Okay, it's not easy, but it's a great talent to develop and use in your personal life. Become a person everyone respects and whose company they enjoy, but also make it clear that when something occurs that you disagree with and concerns you directly, you make a point of mentioning it. Stay clear of power struggles that crop up among colleagues and managers. Supporting one faction or another in office politics is a losing game. If your "side" is victorious, the other side will resent your role. And if your side loses, things will be even worse for you. Work with everyone as needed, refuse to play political games, and focus on the job at hand.

What happens in the office stays in the office.

Never share internal office problems with outsiders, especially clients or suppliers. You gain nothing from gossiping about your employer, and you risk losing respect and confidence among the people you speak to.

Treat the people you work with as friends.

This isn't hard to do. If someone needs a ride home in the rain and you're going their way, offer to take them. Or if you know how to construct a complex chart using Excel and a colleague is having difficulty with it, take time to show them. Think of these gestures as investments. They build capital and support for you among coworkers, lowering the risk that you will become a target of jealousy and gossip.

Never express hostility to a rival.

Some people will regard the target on your back like a red flag to a bull. They'll look for reasons to taunt you as a way of expressing their envy. It's a childish response, but it can get under your skin anyway. What do you do? It's what you *don't* do that matters. Never display an emotional response to their taunts. Keep your cool. Stay above it all. And smile. Smiling can be a wonderful antidote at times like this. It reassures your friends and confuses your enemies.

Remain humble.

Taking pride in your work is great. Using a trumpet to express it is destructive. Accept whatever recognition is awarded by your boss and colleagues, and try not to mention it again, especially in your work environment. If you need more recognition, look for it among your family and friends.

Learn to read people.

This is a skill worth developing, in and out of the business world. It's about observing how people respond in stressful situations. We are all creatures of habit, and we are remarkably predictable when things happen in some circumstances. You can pick up basic secrets from various books on the subject, or you can do it yourself by taking a genuine interest in people around you. Understanding their body language can prepare you for unexpected actions they may take.

Avoid gossip of any kind from anyone.

Remember that jealousy and spreading malicious gossip both grow out of insecurity and that lecturing others about the evils of gossip only creates resentment. Your best response to someone with "hot gossip" for you is to change the subject. If someone spreads malicious stories about another employee, bring up something positive you know about her and her family. Maybe her daughter won a prize at the science fair, or her son is a great guitarist. Mention it in passing. It's an effective way to derail gossip.

Remember the most prized quality in the workplace.

It's loyalty. If you are loyal to your employer and your work colleagues, you gain their loyalty in return. Which means situations where you may have to fend off jealousy, envy, taunts, and gossip won't be a big deal.

TWENTY-FIVE

The Price of Success

Many ideas I have discussed in this book are not entirely original. Psychologists, sociologists, and other students of human behavior have been discussing similar concepts for years. I wanted to explore them here for the practical purpose of explaining the basics of successful selling, and how the same skills are key to building and maintaining personal relationships. This is important to me, because I attribute much of what I have achieved in life to my ability to connect with people on many levels.

My plan in crafting this book was to weave these skills and techniques through the ins and outs of a career in sales. Of all the talents acquired during our lifetime, none is more important than the ability to communicate with people—which, in my opinion, represents the core of all the skills needed to become a successful salesperson. Only by understanding the needs and desires of others, and assisting them to appreciate our own hopes and expectations, can we become truly linked.

Several stories in this book grew out of my participation in *Shark Tank* and my appearances on *Dancing with the Stars.* Like all of life's experiences—good and bad, anticipated and unforeseen—they enriched my life in more ways than I know. I hope you found them interesting. More important, I hope you found them helpful.

I could end my book with the usual summary and review, but I won't. Here's why.

Explaining the role that business has played in my life left little room for me to talk about things that are loosely linked to my message but still worth mentioning. It is impossible, after all, to separate your personal life entirely from your career. It is also foolish to try. Every entrepreneur driven to create a business based on little more than imagination and ambition accepts the fact that he or she must abandon the concept of a fully balanced life. They can never count on arriving home on time for dinner each night, having weekends to themselves, and always being on hand for a child's recital or hockey game.

It's a price most entrepreneurs are willing to pay, and they pay it in multiple ways. Time spent with families becomes limited, so you intensify every moment with them. The demands on your life are made with equal force by both your family obligations and your business interests, so you find a way to satisfy both if possible. Over time, the vision and ambition that drove you to start a business in the beginning can grow fuzzy, so you constantly touch base to remind yourself of your original inspiration.

Easy? It's never easy. It's either vital to you, or it's abandoned. You make the call.

The most demanding aspects of achieving great things as an entrepreneur are the ones that involve family in a positive and rewarding manner. They need recognition and involvement from you as an entrepreneur, and you need their commitment to sharing your goal. You must make it clear, and they must accept that even when it's not apparent you are dedicated to both the business that provides financial security and to the welfare of your family.

It is a difficult high-wire act to perform. If you don't believe the effort is worth the reward, don't even attempt it.

You also need to deal with the same general whirl of life—the small niggles and the major crises—that entangles everyone. You can't escape it. You shouldn't try. Because life will—and *should*—continue to surprise you. Sometimes with pleasure. Sometimes with pain. Successful entrepreneurs need to embrace both. But once again it is difficult. And painful. And unpredictable. I have the scars to prove it.

People like me wish to think we have several lives—business, family, private, public—but in reality we have only one, and it bears no label. We cling to it anyway, because it is the sum of all our experiences in all the personas we choose to adapt.

And in the end, it is all we ever have.

I have spent much of my life pursuing a dream. I continue to pursue the same dream today. The dream does not change, except that it grows bigger and brighter in my mind.

For years I invested massive amounts of time following that dream. I expected my family to understand why it occupied so much of my attention, and I insisted they share the rewards with me. For the most part, they agreed and understood. I tried to balance the ledger by always making a point of seeking unique events to share with them, providing a raft of memories I hoped we would all treasure.

Along with the time I spent with my family, I found ways to keep in touch with the world beyond my office window. After selling the first company I founded, I took three years from business to stay home and care for our youngest daughter until she was old enough to attend school. Later I ran marathons, entered golf tournaments, and raced sports cars on circuits across North America. I enjoyed it all. The marathons, the golf tournaments, and the auto races fed my competitive nature beyond my business activities. They were means of providing me with new experiences, new views of the world, and new ways to wring more joy out of life.

They were also a way of distracting my attention from problems in my personal life. So when my marriage ended abruptly, the emotional impact on me was devastating.

It's a familiar tale, so ageless that it qualifies as a cliché: man at the height of his economic power enjoys celebrity status and material rewards until his personal life collapses, convincing him he is worthless and leading him to ponder suicide. Proving that money cannot buy either happiness or love.

I didn't care about clichés when it happened. I cared only about escaping my pain. I needed to find help from someone wiser in these matters than I, and in search of counsel I approached a priest who was also a family friend. I needed, he agreed, to heal myself, and he suggested the best way to do this would be by helping to heal others. He had an idea of just how I might begin this healing process, and two days later I was flying to Seattle and the Union Gospel Mission. Located in the inner city, the mission is far from the glamour of Seattle's tourist areas. I began my first day there in a kitchen, peeling vegetables for the food line before serving lunch to homeless people. I did the same thing throughout the afternoon and into the evening.

I spent two weeks in Seattle among people whose only possessions were the clothes on their backs, and whose deepest desires were to eat a decent meal, find a safe place to sleep, and someday put a pair of clean socks on their feet.

I was the man who, the previous year, had been overjoyed to learn that the Ferrari motor company was giving me permission to hand over $1.5 million in exchange for an automobile as dramatic in style and advanced in design as the latest jet fighter in the fleet of the U.S. Air Force. Fewer than five hundred of the cars had been built. More than five thousand people wanted and could afford to purchase one.

Twelve months later I was living among people who, in their own way, would appreciate a pair of clean new socks as much as I did my decadent, impractical red LeFerrari car.

How is that for contrast?

TWENTY-SIX

The Significance of Socks

Nothing I confronted during my time at the Union Gospel Mission was familiar to me. Every experience was an education. Until then, I had known little about homeless people except that they needed help. The help, I suspected, should come from within. "The Lord helps those who help themselves," I remembered hearing as a child. The message within it was, *Anyone can lift themselves up by their bootstraps if they try hard enough.* I believed it. Most people do. But then, most people have not spent a week or two in a homeless shelter.

I did not know how badly people lack the means to survive on their own when trapped in a downward spiral of hardship they cannot escape. "Poverty" and "homelessness" had been words to describe someone else's problem in some other world, not my own. It's not that I didn't care about the homeless. It's just that it was all alien to me, and I do not believe this made me that different from the majority of Americans.

Through my time at the mission I was guided by Jeff Lilley, the mission's president. "You're going to see a lot of things here that you never expected to see," Jeff warned me the day I went to work at the admissions desk. "You will encounter addicts, transvestites, and people overdosed on drugs that you have never heard of, and whose effects you could never imagine. You will be among people on the fringes of society, people who appear irrelevant to your life and your values, people you would normally cross the street to avoid. But never, ever judge them. Treat all of them the same way: with love."

His words made me wonder about the idea of helping myself by first helping others. I was still racked with emotional pain, unable to escape it entirely. Would I have a right to feel my pain when dealing with people who often had no idea where they would sleep that night, no idea where they would find something to eat, no idea if they would survive until morning?

When I mentioned this to Jeff, he countered that pain is still pain, no matter who feels it and no matter its cause. Both the pain felt by the people I would be helping and the pain I felt from my marriage failure forged a link between us. The causes were far different. So were the circumstances; I was a temporary visitor to the mission and could leave at any time; the people I would be helping had no alternative, because the mission was often their only lifeline.

"Never mind the differences," Jeff advised me. "You are here to help, and you need help yourself. Everything you do for them will be appreciated and valued. Don't think about your situation or start comparing your life with theirs. Just concentrate on helping and showing them love. That's all any of us can do."

Things did not start off well. A few people I encountered while manning the admissions desk were abusive, physically and verbally. Most were grateful for the help we could offer, but some appeared aggressive and dangerous. They frightened me enough to call 911 and ask for assistance. I called 911 so often that night that a responder finally told me to stay calm, handle the situation on my own, and save them a trip. My concerns began to dissolve when I realized that the people were not angry at me. They were angry and frustrated at the hopelessness of their situation, and I soon understood why.

The men and women who approached the desk were desperate and resigned, with no food to eat and no place to sleep. To them, the world was a dark and unforgiving place until I offered them a meal and a warm bed for the night. That's when they believed the Lord might love them after all, and their existence really had meaning. For one day they could rest, relax, smile, and maybe dream.

Within a few days at the mission, my own sense of worthlessness began to fade. It did not recede entirely; it just became less crippling. Other things were happening. My ego shrank and a sense of humility began growing within me. This sounds like a religious revelation or epiphany, but it was more like a new awareness of what I had done with my life to that point. Jeff explained that it was a common response of people who have achieved material success and chose to leave it behind while they helped people in need of many things, including love.

After a few days among the homeless I realized the changes I was experiencing would remain with me for the rest of my life. I had seen and heard the effects that homelessness has on people—good people, damaged people, needy people, all of them. There would be more to learn and understand about them, but all I had to do to absorb it was remain at the mission.

I was wrong.

When a staff member named Richard suggested I join him on a search-and-rescue trip one night, I agreed to go.

Richard's background was similar to that of many people who worked at the mission. He left home at age fourteen to escape a sexually abusive stepfather and a mother who turned a blind eye to her husband's actions. Having lived on the street, he knew intimately what it was like, how difficult it was to escape, and how much a warm bed and a hot meal were appreciated.

Leaving the mission that night, Richard told me that some homeless people were so far beyond the reach of society they could not make it to the mission. The problem wasn't distance. It was mental. Many had been on their own so long that they were unable to connect with other people in a meaningful way. Along with helping them cope with being homeless, our job would be to show that we knew of their plight and wanted to help them. We would offer them hope that they could build relationships again. Humans are social animals after all, and having no contact with others who care about you is tragic. It is also damaging to your mental health.

Richard warned me that I was about to encounter situations I could not imagine on my own, even after having spent several days at the mission. He was right. When we visited sewer grates, highway underpasses, and other dark corners of the city we found people unable to escape their sadness, pain, and despair. We brought them no lectures, made no appeal for them to change their ways (because we knew they wouldn't), and offered no promises. Instead, we delivered sandwiches, hot cocoa, and assurances that they were loved.

That night, I learned many ways people can be cruel and, thankfully, other ways they can express love and concern for each other. The extremes of both shocked me over and over, despite what I thought I knew about life and relationships. Like the tale of a woman I'll call Susan.

Susan became pregnant by a man she had been living with for some time. The day after she delivered a baby boy, the man visited her in the hospital and said, "Well, he's your problem now." Then he turned and walked away. She never saw or heard from him again, and was discharged from the hospital as a homeless single mother. The man she had counted on for support had abandoned her without a second thought. When I met her and listened to her story, she was living, with her baby, beneath a highway underpass. Hearing her tell her story of what seemed to me unimaginable cruelty, I wanted to comment on the irony of the situation. Dedicating what life she had to her baby, she was telling her story to a man who had pledged he would give his life for his children, although they now wanted nothing to do with him.

I had prepared myself for the sadness and tragedy I encountered at the mission, but Richard was totally correct—the search-and-rescue trip took me to places I could not have imagined on my own. I had not expected the feelings of accomplishment that washed over me simply by handing someone a hot drink and food, and talking with them about whatever they wanted to discuss.

We visited a number of homeless people that night, each grateful for our attention and help. How many? I can't recall. It may have been dozens. It seemed like hundreds.

At about two in the morning, we were preparing to return to the mission when Richard drove past an open field where homeless men often chose to sleep. He suggested we stop and check it out, although it appeared empty.

At first we saw no one, and Richard assumed the men had found another place to go. We were about to leave when I spotted something across the field that looked like a discarded sleeping bag. I walked over to it and noticed blood on the bag, then realized someone was wrapped inside it.

I shouted for Richard, and he and I roused the man inside the bag. He was covered in blood and dirt, and when he woke he said he had been struck by a bus while trying to cross the road. The bus did not stop, and he staggered away to collapse in the field. He knew he would probably die without help, and he did not expect any. He was homeless; unknown; and, he believed, without love. All he could do was wrap himself in the sleeping bag and wait to die. God, he believed, had abandoned him.

"Why would you think that?" Richard asked.

The man told us that he had ruined his life. "I've done terrible things," he said. "I'm worthless. I have nothing left to give."

Richard and I assured him that God never abandoned people, and that someone was always available to help him, no matter who he was or what he might have done.

The man was not as badly injured as we first feared. We managed to sit him up and help him drink cocoa. Then, with Richard and I supporting him, we helped the man to his feet, and the three of us stood holding hands and praying. It was a remarkable experience. We saw that he received proper medical attention, wished him well, and headed back to the mission.

After ten days at the mission I was ready to go forward with my life, wherever it led. I don't know if my efforts had helped any of the homeless people I had met, but I knew that parts of me had begun to heal, and I was ready to resume doing things I enjoyed, things that mattered to me and to others.

My education at the mission revealed many things to me. All were meaningful, and many were surprising. Among them was an appreciation for the importance of small things to people who lacked so much. Like fresh, clean socks. Warm coats, sweaters, and hats are always appreciated by the homeless, but nothing is more valued than a pair of new socks. Having brand-new socks is a brief luxury to them, but a luxury nonetheless.

People with a home, a sense of self-worth, and a drawer full of clothes are not able to understand the appeal of pulling a pair of new socks over weary and calloused feet. After days and nights spent among homeless at the mission, I understood the luxury of it. I decided to mark my time there by providing that small pleasure regularly. No one has the power, financial or otherwise, to solve the problem of homelessness on his own—not on a national level and not even for Seattle. But something could be done on a smaller yet significant scale.

If a pair of new socks could make the homeless at the mission feel better about themselves, I could do something about it. The day before I left, Richard and I headed for a nearby Wal-Mart, where we bought every pair of adult socks in the store. We filled eight shopping carts, lined up at the checkout counter to pay for them, and headed back to the mission, where they were handed out to every homeless person there.

I didn't want anyone at the mission to know the source of the socks. I just wanted them to enjoy the luxury of putting them on and know that someone valued them enough to provide a pair of new socks even if they had difficulty valuing themselves. When I returned home, I arranged with a sock manufacturer to ship thousands of pairs of new socks to the mission every three months.

Leaving the mission, I thanked every staff member I encountered there for their patience, their understanding, and the privilege of sharing with me all the things they do each day of the year. I told them they were fortunate to be doing what they do, and I meant it.

During my time at the mission I grew connected to humanity

in ways I could never have imagined. People who rise from hardship to achieve wealth and fame had been my heroes and my models. They still are, in their own way. In Seattle, I acquired new heroes of a special breed—people such as Jeff and Susan and Richard and many others. Back home I was once again among wealth and comfort far beyond their imagining. Yet, in a spiritual sense, I identified them as my brothers and sisters, and still do. They cannot live my life, and I cannot live theirs. But together we had forged a link between us that had nothing to do with material wealth and everything to do with understanding what it is to be human and to feel pain and loss.

I mentioned this to Jeff as I was leaving. His response was to tell me he understood my reaction and to say that he had never found anything more fascinating than another human being.

His words changed my thinking about life, and the change was massive.

Once, I believed there was no such thing as a victim. Each of us, I assumed, can do whatever it takes to pull ourselves out of any situation we find ourselves in. We only need to try hard enough; we only need to want it badly enough. That doesn't work for me anymore. It's why I make it a point to speak to every homeless person I meet. I listen to their stories. I help where I can. I remind myself that everyone has a lesson to share with the world, and that the world should listen and care. Especially care.

During the first few weeks after returning from Seattle, the word that began filling my consciousness was *enrichment*, the sense of confirming our worth as individuals and justifying our presence on earth.

We all need someone to enrich our lives.

I found mine while dancing.

TWENTY-SEVEN

Keep Moving Forward

I recall reading a magazine article that pointed out how our personal character is shaped not as much by our accomplishments as by the setbacks we face in "the crucibles of challenge."

I like that phrase: *the crucibles of challenge*. It confirms that none of us can avoid setbacks and failure from time to time. Since we can't avoid failure, we should prepare ourselves to learn from it.

Most failures occur when we stretch ourselves beyond our limits, striving to achieve a new performance level in business or sports or some other endeavor. Failure at that point will do one of two things to us: it will either force us to cower in a safe place where comfort becomes more important than achievement, or it will stretch the limits of our ambition, inspiring us to apply the lessons we learned from the failure.

I'm all for learning and not cowering.

Talking about the upside of failure is relatively new in America. This is, after all, where we expect to realize our dreams through diligence and effort, and our ambition is restricted only by self-doubt. For the most part, this is true. But it's a mistake to believe there is never room for failure in that promise.

It was important for me to mention two events in this book

that have little direct connection with the art of selling but much to do with life in general—mine and, in one form or another, everyone else's. One was my agreement to take part in *Dancing with the Stars,* where I pushed myself well past my level of reasonable expectations. I had never danced before and I was older than most of the other contestants. Still, I expected to learn something about myself, and I did.

The other was the end of my marriage. No matter how you deal with it, a divorce is a symbol of failure. My emotional reaction to it inspired me to heal myself by helping to heal others. I could not have imagined experiencing this on my own and, while I mourn the end of my marriage, my time at the Union Gospel Mission changed me in ways that I will always value.

Sometimes, among the dark and dingy corners of failure, we discover light flashing from a source we never knew about. This happened to me when, after pushing aside feelings of depression that still lingered after I returned from the mission, I agreed to take part in *Dancing with the Stars.* I was paired with Kym Johnson, whom I knew nothing about at the time. Kym became my professional dancing partner, filling the role from the first day with warm humor, great wisdom, splendid grace, and infinite patience. As weeks passed, Kym became more than my partner on the dance floor. She became my source of happiness and joy at a level I had not experienced for a very long time. This book is not about Kym; it is about my advice and encouragement to you in choosing a career as a professional salesperson. But none of it would unfold in the manner it has without Kym in my life.

One more story about a wise and strong woman:

Her name was Mary, and she lived a difficult yet rewarding life. Just out of her teens in the late 1930s, Mary and her young husband moved to a small farm on the northern Prairies. The land was hardscrabble and the farm had no indoor plumbing. For many years, the family's income depended more on Mary's salary from teaching in a small country schoolhouse than on anything they earned from the crops they managed to harvest.

When all their children were grown and gone, Mary and her husband sold their farm and settled in town. Mary had always wanted to visit their daughter, who had moved to California, and shortly after her seventieth birthday Mary decided that she and her husband would drive across the country to visit her that summer.

Their children tried to talk her out of it. It was a very long drive, they reminded her. At their age driving that distance was too dangerous. They should fly to California, not try to drive there. Mary's response to their concerns was her usual, "Nonsense." She and her husband had been unable to travel when raising a family and running the farm. Now they would get a chance to see part of the country they had never visited before. She hated flying, and the road trip would be relaxing and educational. Her children were well acquainted with their mother's stubbornness. They stopped haranguing her and gathered to wave good-bye as their parents drove off. Headed west.

On the second day of the trip, while Mary was driving and her husband dozed in the seat beside her, Mary lost control of the car. It struck a tree at high speed before rolling into a ditch. Mary's husband was killed instantly, and Mary spent months recuperating in the hospital. She was reminded several times by the doctors and nurses that she was lucky to survive the accident. Only her stubborn disposition, they surmised, had driven her to recover.

When she returned home, she remained silent, almost morose, for some time. She blamed herself for their father's death, she explained to her children. Now she wanted to be left alone with her thoughts.

But soon she was herself again. She moved with difficulty, but by Christmas she had all the energy and mobility she'd had when her children were scampering in and out of the house. All through Christmas and into the New Year she baked pies and prepared casseroles for her children, made clothes for her grandchildren, and resumed her social activities with friends.

Everyone was pleased and astounded by her recovery, both physical and mental. After her near-death experience at the wheel of the car and accepting responsibility for her husband's death, Mary lived a fulfilling and vibrant twenty-five more years before dying in her sleep at age ninety-six.

The entire town paid tribute to Mary at her memorial service, many of them remembering the woman who had returned from the accident that killed her husband and left her with a permanent limp. At the service her eldest son told those gathered that he had been as mystified as anyone, and had once asked her, "Mom, how did you do it? How did you lift yourself out of all that misery?"

He told everyone that his mother replied, "I told myself, 'Listen, you've got to start moving forward. You can't go back, and there's no sense in standing still. So you start moving forward and you keep moving forward.' That's what it takes. That's what I did. I decided to just keep moving forward."

I have had my disappointments and my setbacks in the past, and I expect I'll deal with some in the future. When I do, I'll try to remember Mary's line,

Just keep moving forward.

It's the only way to go.